Resistance in Colonial and Communist China, 1950–1963

T0383672

The history of colonial East Asia is a human anatomy describing beneficial organs of foreign rule. Proclaiming itself a schematic diagram open to inspection, the anatomy of the late British Empire nevertheless obscured much more than it revealed. This analogy in Price's provocative Cold War history is not presented only as an insight on imperialism but deciphers competing nationalist ideologies, too. The Kuomintang contended vigorously against communist rule in southern China for a decade after the end of the civil war in 1949 and Chinese communists disparaged British colonialism in Hong Kong in a war of words peaking in 1956–1957. These clashes of will did not produce new rulers in either place. They informed a period of Sino-British strategic partnership based on recognition that a capitalist enclave in southern China had its uses.

By focusing on the Hong Kong region, *Resistance in Colonial and Communist China* compares anatomies of the British colonial government, the Chinese communists and stateless members of the remnant Kuomintang (1950–1963). Price asserts that after 1949, the colonial government of Hong Kong politically favoured the Kuomintang organised crime societies over their communist nationalist adversaries despite historiographical explanation that it favoured neither.

This book challenges traditional concepts of the British colonial government and its attitude towards communist China. It engages in current debates surrounding Britain's past by presenting a particularly devious episode of late colonial history.

R.B.E. Price is a Lecturer-at-Law at Southern Cross University, Australia and has held visiting professorships across China. His other publications include *Reading Colonies: Property and Control of the British Far East* (2016, City University Press of Hong Kong), the biography of a Hong Kong land officer, *Going Native: The Passions of Philip Jacks* (2016, Australian Scholarly Publishing) and *Violence and Emancipation in Colonial Ideology* (forthcoming). His current project is a theoretical work, 'On Occupation'.

Resistance in Colonial and Communist China, 1950–1963

Anatomy of a Riot

R.B.E. Price

Routledge
Taylor & Francis Group

LONDON AND NEW YORK

First published 2019
by Routledge
2 Park Square, Milton Park, Abingdon, Oxon OX14 4RN

and by Routledge
52 Vanderbilt Avenue, New York, NY 10017

First issued in paperback 2020

Routledge is an imprint of the Taylor & Francis Group, an informa business

© 2019 R.B.E. Price

British Library Cataloguing-in-Publication Data
A catalogue record for this book is available from the British Library

Library of Congress Cataloging-in-Publication Data
Names: Price, Rohan, author.
Title: Resistance in colonial and communist China
  (1950–1963).
Description: Abingdon, Oxon ; New York, NY : Routledge,
  2019. | Includes bibliographical references and index.
Identifiers: LCCN 2018047700 | ISBN 9781138388857
  (hardback) | ISBN 9780429424335 (ebook)
Subjects: LCSH: Hong Kong (China)–History–20th century. |
  Hong Kong (China)–Politics and government–20th century. |
  Great Britain–Colonies–Asia–Administration. | China–Foreign
  relations–Great Britain. | Great Britain–Foreign relations–China.
Classification: LCC DS796.H757 P75 2019 |
  DDC 951.2505–dc23
LC record available at https://lccn.loc.gov/2018047700

ISBN 13: 978-0-367-67033-7 (pbk)
ISBN 13: 978-1-138-38885-7 (hbk)

Typeset in Galliard
by Apex CoVantage, LLC

Contents

Abbreviations

CCP	Chinese Communist Party
CIA	Central Intelligence Agency
CPG	Chinese People's Government
CPSU	Communist Party of the Soviet Union
HMG	Her Majesty's Government
KIS	Kuomintang Intelligence Service
KMT	Kuomintang
KSJP	*Kung-shang Jih-pao* newspaper
PLA	People's Liberation Army
SCMP	*South China Morning Post* newspaper
SoSC	Secretary of State for the Commonwealth

Preface

The civil war in China did not end neatly on 1 October 1949. Political and militant resistance to communism was a strong pulse of southern China's history in the period between 1950 and 1963. Colonialism was resisted too. Chinese communist post-riot criticisms of the inadequate and biased compensation practices of British colonialism in Hong Kong in 1957 is one example. Another example was afforded by Leftist protests at the colony's indifference to Chinese Nationalist sabotage raids in the new communist republic throughout the late 1950s.

Whether cold war conflict found outlet in a heated war of words between familiar sparring partners or came in a message sent to claim responsibility for a bomb detonated in a railway station, there were conventions to textual and spoken violence – for example, what a party said was not a reliable indicator of who it was. I say this is a general principle, before any particular exegesis can begin or the officeholders in the history clubhouse confirm the minutes of their AGM. Colonialism, communism and bourgeois nationalism each had an anatomy that disguised underlying realities – in the form of a hidden constituency of private motives projecting an objective political aim. This is my central claim.

This history tries to unravel the private motives of nationalism. In doing so, I wing my way through a no-fly zone clouded by Kuomintang (KMT) diatribe and Chinese Communist (CCP) distortions and land my own motive in a barely free land where things colonisers can never bring themselves to admit are spoken about openly and fervently by locals. It is as if the Indian Mutiny retaliations, the starvation of Bengal, hunting the Mau Mau, the dispersals of South East Queensland, massacres at Batang Kali, Amritsar and Myall Creek all happened in one town, in the same country, yesterday. Refuelling on this high-octane rage, I fly on – my only aims are to reach altitude and describe the difference between mountains and seas below. How could anyone not know the difference? I only record the obvious vistas sprawling and abutting below me because we have lost our habit of arguing about topography as new or ancient, in tectonic tension, as enemies crumbling enemies, or skidding lightly enough to co-exist in the same world.

My choice of the word 'anatomy' is purposeful. Yet what does the word 'anatomy' bring to mind? Perhaps one thinks of a branch of biology dedicated to depicting human organs in cross-section or relief illustrations? The product of centuries of dissection, anatomy is a science of show and tell about the human body. What needs to be known is in plain sight. A colonial history claims an authoritative ground. Like a medical anatomy, it acknowledges no variation to its schema of the body, views its processes as verified and routine, and regards empiricism not as a dialectical smash of knowledges but as a tightly refereed corridor.

An anatomy of a colonial riot dispassionately projected characteristics such as state authority, compensative function and due process in a manner immune to questions or doubt. Perceived by the public to be a product of an official process, it gave comfort and relief. It encouraged skepticism; it was not the object of it. Although anatomy was always a front, one must be less than sanguine on what its insight implies. Even if another history can be proven, submerged beneath anatomy's carapace of shine and denial, and even if its apologists have a conscience, they will not adjust their story. The aim of this text is to offer hope to a fresh historiography, not to beg acceptance of a pimple on the colonial anatomy.

These pages vivisect colonial Hong Kong's grandest claim: its scions of Albion faithfully maintained neutrality towards both the CCP and KMT nationalists provided that neither broke local law and order protocols. This view has been fanned into a steady torch by Norman Miners: 'communist China could live with a colony ruled by British administrators but would not long have tolerated one which offered opportunities for its political opponents to attain power'.[1] This claim makes no comment on evidence presented in these pages of KMT militants using Hong Kong as a base for United States-funded terror raids in southern China for over a decade dating from 1950. It also misleads by *oublie commodément*. The colonial response to Hong Kong's 1956 'Double Ten' riot carefully selected KMT-aligned businesses to compensate, laughed in the faces of communist loss, and ensured KMT rioters escaped British justice, such as it was.

The recognitions between British colonial authorities and the bourgeois Chinese gangster set in Hong Kong are ignored by a naïve academic literature disclaiming their political connections and sticking to a story of observed formalities. In the post-civil war years between 1951 to 1954, Chinese triad society membership blossomed to an estimated 300, 000 members, up to a tenth of whom made Hong Kong the epicentre of their global operations.[2] As Ko-Lin Chin put it, 'Chinese organised crime gangs . . . initially formed not to commit crime but to achieve a political or social goal'.[3] Ties of kinship and commercial purpose meant that triad organisations and their members traversed lines of legality, as well as colonial and anti-colonial politics. It made many ethical distinctions about their activities in the realm of British colonialism in Hong Kong rather lacking in normative anchor points.

As one 1960s commentator put it: 'the step from the Triad Society to the Kuomintang . . . is very short'.[4] This being the case, any pattern disclosing the British administration's support for KMT-aligned business figures necessarily also supported the funding of mainland reprisal and retribution raids on communist targets. It sounds fanciful to claim an over-policed state such as colonial Hong Kong could not be expected to properly monitor and prevent Hong Kong-based KMT adventurism across the border. Yet that was exactly what colonial authorities claimed.

The British anatomy claimed equality in how commercial policy was applied in Hong Kong. The boast had to cover more than a few distortions. For example, a little more than half of the total 1957 riot compensation payments of HK$1,478,965 was made to the Garden Confectioners and Bakers Company.[5] Its Shamshui Po factory and headquarters were ransacked and destroyed by rioters on 11 October 1956. Other factories and business premises were destroyed as well, but the British administration compensated only those in its preference. This company, awarded a towering sum of HK$743,000, was owned by cousins and KMT military-industrial yes-men to the British, Tse Fong Cheung and Wah O. Wong,[6] who reputedly followed Yang Yongtai's Politics Research Group. Garden Company had procured a contract in the early 1930s to supply the KMT's Southern Army with bread. It had a reputation for making confectionary and baked items that most people, including peddlers and cardboard collectors, could afford. Hence, it made good sense for the food security of Hong Kong to get the Garden Company factory up and running again. But it was equally consistent with rewarding KMT businessmen for a history of not making waves locally whilst supporting their mainland political allies.

Post-war colonialism was not a distributive physiology. It might have been a fantasy stippled by bad conscience, or a case of keeping the class at their desks for two decades after the final bell, but it distributed nothing of consequence. What its anatomy presented was an attuned corpus of civilisation and economic co-development. Yet it could never be a representative diagram of rudely circulated, widespread progress. Institutional racism and indifference to refugee squalor nearly always put paid to that in southern China. The only concern of the British government of Hong Kong was to prevent its economy's organ failure. This was ensured by keeping the investment of the KMT – triadic at its core and nervy in its affiliations – flowing into their colony during the post-war reconstruction years. It also wanted to keep Hong Kong out of the thoughts of John Foster Dulles and the U.S. State Department whenever possible, while keeping Peking's communists at bay by offering them a measure of freedom to buy and sell in Hong Kong. The communists were big spenders in Hong Kong. They sloshed their reserves all around the banking system.

The colonial government was covertly supportive of the KMT through an asymmetrical policy offering succour to KMT militant remnants in Hong Kong on the pretext of an open border policy with China. After mistakenly pursuing a policy of too strongly holding communists accountable for the riot of 1956, the colonial government used high-profile prosecution of Nationalist militants in Hong Kong in 1963 as a pressure valve dispersing tension with communist China.

One might expect the fraught position of the British in Hong Kong after the Second World War to be downplayed in the colony's historical accounts. My problem with the view of Miners was that it went too far. He insisted on preaching an imperial line of Hong Kong being independent of China by the necessity of its own survival. Unfortunately, this feeds a false reading of history that imagines Hong Kong as some sort of independent state: a part of China because of the cross-border sojourning of its Chinese people but aloof and colonial in ways that more greatly mattered. This might have described the situation in 1949. In 1963 it became nonsense. American State Department suspicions about unhelpful British motives in Hong Kong toward the KMT peaked in 1963 when British Foreign Office correspondence questioned whether American truculence towards it was 'deliberately' intended to sour relations between Whitehall and Taipei further.[7]

The communists responded angrily to the colonial government including them in the blame for the 1956 Hong Kong riot. This formed a ratcheting point in already tense Sino-British relations. The prosecution in Hong Kong of the mainland saboteurs from the KMT in 1963 stands as an extraordinary example of the British colonial administration relinquishing the fortunes of the colony to the communist sphere of influence. Some of my colleagues in history will say this is wrong or not properly evidenced. Raising the prospect seems a small price to pay for encouraging scholarship on why the fragile colonial Cold War grasp on Hong Kong should matter to free peoples today.

Lao Tzu once asked: 'is it not because he who is without thought of self is able to accomplish his private ends?'[8] A view of altruism as selfishness can be no surprise to students of colonialism or its anatomy. When applied to the crony circle around a governor in a British East Asian colony in the post-war years, the corruption, or subjectivity of a policy's impact, had to be obscured by claiming to serve a polity other than itself or British share-holders. Lao Tzu contended one hand washing the other was an eternal truth. It also informed how colonial governments out East spread money around.

The compensation payments made in 1957 by British colonial authorities after the 1956 Hong Kong riot show how well members of the KMT pliant to colonialism could do, and especially so when claims for communist losses were denied. For example, the Canton Metal Window Manufacturing Company factory in Shamshui Po was badly damaged in the riot, and it was the second-largest recipient of compensation with a government payout of $476,000,[9] allowing it to relocate to new premises in Kwun Tong in 1960. Officers of this company wrote the public submission to the compensation commission on behalf of the Chinese General Chamber of Commerce[10] – Hong Kong's most solicitous colonial society for KMT businesspeople. By making the correlation between compensation payments and bourgeois Nationalist beneficiaries evident, the British colonial modus in Hong Kong, and elsewhere in the eastern Empire, can be revealed as a history lurking behind an anatomical facade.

The private ends of colonial capitalism were the reality beneath its prosperity claims of a circulative anatomy to the benefit of an entire corpus. Colonial rulers used compensation benevolence, and criminal justice lenience, to create subjects of goodwill that could be counted on in the future. Richard Cobb, writing in the *Times Literary Supplement* in the 1960s, observed that 'a man who describes himself as a wine merchant when caught in a riot may, at other times of day, be a clerk, a brothel keeper or a riverside worker'.[11] A rioter could also be called 'a wine merchant' by a colonial government counting how much was lost in broken bottles.

This text makes no secret of inciting readers to examine their assumptions about southern China history. In 1963, the British colonial authorities started prosecuting KMT militants discovered in possession of explosives in Hong Kong. This made me curious as to why. After going soft on the KMT after the Double Ten riot and caring little about post-civil war use of Hong Kong by Nationalist militants as a refuge, it seemed an unusual turn of events. Almost overnight, the era of indifference by the British toward the KMT's violence was replaced by a pro-Chinese communist policy *against* KMT militants. When I say it made me curious, I mean, suspicious.

There was a broader stage for the events described here. By the end of 1960 through its organ *Pravda*, the Russian government openly called Chinese communists 'dogmatists and extremists'.[12] The Chinese began competing with the Russians openly in diplomatic matters in the Third World. The Chinese government became increasingly cooperative with Whitehall in the early 1960s in their dealings over Hong Kong and its practical problems including the colony's unreliable water supply. By the late 1950s, due to the end of the Sino-Russian friendship period, the British had finally found their métier in Cold War ideological posturing: they were the capitalist free port enclave owners who knew where the mark lay and did not overstep it.

The KMT policy had shifted to *contra*. Anatomical bluffing nevertheless continued to rib a heart of imperial hubris. In 1963, for example, the British governing clique in Hong Kong began claiming that they were not doing the bidding of the communists but acting on recent revelations concerning the scourge of KMT terrorism in southern China.[13] Such inconsistency demonstrated that the British administration in Hong Kong seldom held a pious middle ground. To borrow a less dignified Chinese analogy, it zipped like a shuttlecock from one side of the net to the other.

So, what is this book trying to do? **Chapter 1** contends that the communist anatomy in southern China was conflicted between its colonial admiration and commitment to anti-Rightist purging. Until the riot of 1956, the communist ambivalence to capitalism generally distracted them from raising British support for KMT militants using the colony as a base for sabotage raids into mainland China. **Chapter 2** deepens the analysis of the British colonial anatomy by describing what the Hong Kong riot of 1956 revealed about its use of criminal justice settings to deflect attention from the KMT and toward bystanders and communists. **Chapter 3** explains the Chinese communist-British colonial detente against the KMT in 1963 as pragmatic symbolism. **Chapter 4** compresses KMT, Chinese communist and British colonial anatomies in the southern China context to glimpse the realities that lay beneath the song and dance put on by each.

Chapter 5 situates Hong Kong in a broader canvass of historical influences, including the colonial desire to always be a step ahead in the technology game. It concludes that the techniques of every anatomy, colonial or otherwise, settled the same questions concerning access to intellectual products and the bounty of modernity. By not bringing in technology unless it improved cost efficiency, or bringing it in and hogging the proceeds, the colonial moment relied heavily on cheap 'machine hand' labour to create colonial hierarchy. This occurred not in an outwardly discriminatory basis, but by letting white indivisibility from its technology do the social ordering. After 1949, the communist Chinese had their own set of issues over mothballed and make-do technology and its lack of utility to Red-thinking. It extruded instead in bad films about growing turnips under the party's leadership and harnessing the easy gain capitalism of Hong Kong, learning along the way to enjoy its speakeasy and hairdresser familiarity, and huckster energy, with no risk to their communist souls. They were made impervious by incantations of history practised in the bathroom mirror for sincerity and projection of humanist appeal.

The anatomy of a riot occurred through a perfect coordination of institutions. The anatomy allowed no view except an official one. Nevertheless, anatomising was not only for those in power. Communist and bourgeois nationalist projections were at the heart of an anatomy espoused by each. Ideology could not be slapped on so thickly, or call earnestly down to the lowest subject with a vision for their redemption, unless there was received purity in a clinician's command to subjects. Derived from a political monopoly, it called on subjects to compete with each other or join up selflessly with them in a common fate. Differences between the philosophies does not make them incomparable by reference to anatomical techniques.

This text presumes to introduce a fresh lineage into the Cold War historiography of Hong Kong and southern China. Yet it also has something to say about ideology and the souls of the people subject to colonial capitalism, bourgeois republicanism and communism. The faithful followers of each anatomy have enjoyed a privileged place in history. Those who regarded the anatomies as a sham were ignored. Their voices are heard here.

Notes

1 Norman Miners, 'Plans for Constitutional Reform in Hong Kong 1946–1952 and 1984–1989' *Asian Journal of Public Administration* vol. 11, no. 1 (1997): 471.
2 K. Bolton and C. Hutton, *Triad Societies: Triad Societies in Hong Kong* (London: Taylor & Francis, 2000), 83.
3 Letizia Paoli, *The Oxford Handbook to Organised Crime* (Oxford: Oxford University Press, 2014), 224.
4 Anthony Brown, 'The Societies Specialise in Violence' *The Canberra Times* (7 August 1964), 2.
5 HKRS 163-1-2029 (294/57): 'Payment Arrangements for Riot Compensation'.
6 Industrial History Group, 'Industrial History of Hong Kong' website. Avail. at: https://industrialhistoryhk.org/garden-company-%E5%98%89%E9%A0%93%E6%9C%89%E9%99%90%E5%85%AC%E5%8F%B8-founded-1926/ (accessed 10 August 2018).
7 HKRS 158-1-283: 'E.G. Willan to CM MacLehose' (28 June 1963), [2]. These tensions are further explored in chapter 3. Note also: the HKRS 158 file containing riot correspondence appears under a folder label 'Foreign Office Far Eastern Dept 1954–6 Disturbances in Kowloon (Disturbances, Riots and Incidents) 440/01' but only the archive reference no., telegram or letter title and date will be used, not this longer designation.
8 Lao Tzu, *Tao Te Ching* (London: Penguin Classics, 1963), 11.
9 HKRS163-1-2029 (294/57): 'Payment Arrangements for Riot Compensation'.
10 American Consulate General, *Chinese Press Review* (Hong Kong: American Consulate General, 1956), 19.

11 Cited in Keith Flett (ed), *A History of Riots* (Newcastle: Cambridge Scholars Publishing, 2015), 3.
12 CIA-RDP78-03061A000100020014-5: 'The Sino-Soviet Dispute as Seen by Pietro Nenni and the PSI' in 'Bi-Weekly Propaganda Guidance No. 53' (21 November 1960), 1.
13 HKMS 158-1-283: Reuters Report: 'Saboteurs Have Been Working Through Hong Kong in Recent Months – Hau Sang Case' (30 July 1963), [1].

1 Communist anatomy (1950–1955)

Introduction

In 1948, Hong Kong's Governor Alexander Grantham coined a tenuous refrain that the Kuomintang (KMT), just like the communists, was equally on notice in the colony: 'action will be taken impartially against any Chinese individuals or political parties whose activities are detrimental to the law and order of the colony'.[1] Yet the main concern for the British colonial government was how to cater to the interests of its commercially minded partners in the KMT, flecked as they were by money laundering mobsters and holders of other corruptly gained commercial permissions, without unnecessarily offending the communist government of China.

This chapter offers a survey of the social and political conditions of Hong Kong and southern China that challenged the ideological anatomies of Chinese communism and British colonialism. The Chinese Communist Party (CCP) discovered in the wake of the 1956 riot that its enjoyment of Hong Kong's liberal conditions had weakened its anti-colonial anatomy. What it saw as the alliance of the Americans, British and the KMT only made matters worse. Since 1950, Mao Tse-tung had insisted that the British government retract from its relationship with the 'Kuomintang remnant of reactionaries' in Hong Kong, and elsewhere, as a condition of mutual diplomatic recognition.[2] It dawned on the British government led by Harold Macmillan that, after its recognition of the People's Republic of China, the communist Chinese were not going to forget its acceptance of this condition.

The anatomy presented by the communist Chinese in Hong Kong had been manicured to maintain commercial access to the British colony. Their resistance to the colonial narrative only sharpened noticeably in Hong Kong 1947 and 1956–1957. The party demonstrated an anatomy of non-critique and promoted a period of calm between these years. Occasional communist protests received a sharp colonial retort reminding the CCP of how much freedom of commercial action it took for granted in Hong Kong. The CCP was also incidentally reminded by such diatribes that, beyond notional equality in business freedom, there were causes for its complaint not addressed by colonial authorities, including their permission for outrages performed by remnant bourgeois nationalists on the soil of communist southern China from bases in Hong Kong.

Anatomical appearances given by British recognition for the communist government of China, although misleading, were nevertheless commonly thought at the time to carry risks. *New Statesman* journalist Lois Michison gave an account of the 1956 riot as the kind of trouble British authorities were particularly worried about, as the aim of the KMT 'was to provoke Peking by attacks on local communists into invading Hong Kong and triggering off a world war'.[3] This, she reasoned, was the only way Chiang Kai-shek could get the naval and air support from the United States necessary to recover a footing in mainland China.[4] Yet the KMT central committee in Taipei never risked making British Hong Kong the site of a world war or a briefly overheated corner of the Cold War. The colony was a perfect example of 'any harbour in a storm' to its desperate off-scourings. The party's resistance activities across the border in China at times cut across Whitehall enjoying a workable relationship with the communist Chinese. Yet its ambitions after 1949 seldom rose much above playing out its hand for a chance at U.S. approval and the opportunity to squander its funding.

Let us first consider the compromised anatomical position of communist resistance to colonial rule in Hong Kong in the early 1950s. Then I will describe how conditions in communist mainland China, and continued acts of KMT defiance there, shaped the policies and aspirations of parties in Hong Kong. When, in 1956, Zhou Enlai protested against British colonial indifference to 'cold blooded murder and looting by KMT agents',[5] he affirmed that a fundamental role of the state – whether colonial or communist – was to save itself by using its exceptional powers to maintain law and order. No-one could challenge the qualification of the CCP to say this after the example of the KMT insurrections it put down without mercy in 1950–1951 in neighbouring Guangdong.

There was also an element of self-rebuke in Zhou's comment. A government should accept its role in creating conditions causing reactionary behaviour. It followed Mao's thoughts on certain disturbances in mainland China in 1956 properly being blamed not on the frustration of agricultural cooperatives but on bureaucracy on the part of the leadership, and their lack of educational work among the peasants.[6] It was a rare example of communist anatomy and underlying reality being aligned. More arguably, Zhou's comment lit a slow-burning fuse that would lead to the Cultural Revolution-inspired unrest in Hong Kong in 1967, which British appeasements stiffening Hong Kong border control in 1962, and KMT prosecutions in 1963, could not stave off.

Serving as an introduction to the riot of 1956, this chapter investigates two issues: (1) the reasons why communist anti-colonialism resistance remained generally muted in Hong Kong from 1947 until 1956 and (2) inconsistencies in the CCP anatomy caused by its Old Society carnage in the southern provinces of China (1950–1951). In the case of the CCP, Hong Kong's value to it as a stable resort of commercial calm put pressing colonial authorities on KMT activities relatively low on their agenda for most of the 1950s. The CCP seeking such an objective in Hong Kong weakened its anti-colonial anatomy until 1956 when it was reinvigorated by the riots. This was the case although the CCP's anti-foreignism intensified in the form of anti-Rightist and anti-capitalist purges on home soil (1950–1951).

Colonial recognitions

The Chinese Communist Party had a big problem in southern China in 1950. It needed capitalist Hong Kong to remain a stable port for use as an import hub for non-combat materials including vehicles, medical goods, foodstuffs and building materials bound for the war effort on the Korean peninsula. This meant that, for at least as long as the Korean War continued, the CCP had to tread warily on the issue of Hong Kong returning to its fold. Their statements insisting that Hong Kong, Kowloon and the New Territories be returned to Mother China became less frequent, or as Loh put it, the CCP 'took care not to challenge British sovereignty' because 'its Liberal political environment provided significant strategic value'.[7]

In contrast to 1950s, the CCP in the final few years of the civil war had not been restrained at all in expressing its resistance to British rule. The agenda of a meeting of local communists in Hong Kong in 1947 declared these items as their battlefronts:

> Immediate withdrawal of US troops from China,[8] the return to China of Hong Kong and Kowloon, cessation of hostilities in China and cooperation with Chinese students abroad.[9]

Surprising uses were found for such agendas in post-war Hong Kong. When the British colonial government of Hong Kong blamed both the KMT and the Chinese communists for creating the riot strife of 1956, it seemed to take quite a gamble in putting nationalist politics at the heart of the riot. Yet it was the latent nature of communist resistance to British rule that made a narrative of their violent antagonism quite easy to fabricate in times of social or economic disturbance.

The Chinese communists could have easily expelled the British from Hong Kong at any point in the 1950s. They should not have taken the colonial blame for the riot of 1956 as badly as they did. They were febrile about it. They were compelled to a mixed metaphor: 'the Hong Kong authorities are playing with fire and juggling on a very dangerous road'.[10] The agencies of the Chinese communist government in Hong Kong had demonstrably maintained restraint throughout the riot, although its buildings and papers had been burned in it, and its people stabbed in the street. However, in the aftermath of the riot, the communists noted that KMT rioters, including those accused of murder or assault, including many cases of vicious assault, had initial sentences lightened or simply remained at large.[11]

The popular media was not necessarily at odds with communist concerns. It took no effort to downplay Hong Kong as a triad town. One article estimated that there were upwards of 20,000 'hardcore Triad men' in Hong Kong in 117 societies.[12] Having realised the motive of the British for spreading the blame for the riots had been to keep KMT supporters out of jail, local communists asked: 'would [the British] prefer we join in a fight?' and 'would the Hong Kong authorities also like America to join in?'[13]

Like Western alarmism about Hong Kong, communist catastrophism seemed to have a reason. Since 1949, a vein of CCP strategic thought suspected the safety of Hong Kong to its members. The wives and extended family of senior local apparatchiks numbering two hundred people left the colony by boat in May 1949 as they were 'impressed by [the] warning' that 'a third world war was going to begin in the near future'.[14] The chief spouse Madame Tsai Ting-kai 'departed hastily' with her family, however, and at odds with her husband's instructions, did not sell their house.[15] In November 1950, communist civic cadres in the districts of Tungkuan and Paon – just across the border from Hong Kong's New Territories – told the local populace that 'Hong Kong will be liberated' and that civilian labour drafting was needed for the construction of an airfield at nearby Houhai.[16] Such actions as pre-emptive protection of local communists from internment and facilitating troop deployment near the border were preparatory acts, not acts of war. Nevertheless, such scares rippled through the colony quite often.

Other accounts have viewed Hong Kong in the post-war period from the point of view of the communist leadership in the Guangdong, operatives Xinhua News/Bank of China and the State Council's Foreign Affairs Office. Nothing has been written about the communist ontology in Hong Kong visible in the practice of its agents in commercial and street politics. Who were the party members at risk of being shot or stabbed in the generally not investigated tit-for-tat fights between the KMT and the CCP? Who were the ones who did the business of communists in the colony? In CIA accounts, communists straddled their politics and business interests with ease. They shared a similar disfigurement too.

Long-faced communists

A rather comical aspect of a CIA report on Hong Kong communist activities in the early 1950s was that three out of the five main agents were described as having 'high cheekbones' or 'long faces'.[17] The agent most frequently associated with rabble-rousing in the Hong Kong and southern China area was Lao Ying, who was described as 'a trusted representative of Mao-tse Tung and an important official on a policy-making level'.[18] Lao was responsible for appointments to the Canton council. In addition to his responsibilities for authorising political violence and liaison with Peking, he was also something of a dandy. He sported western clothes and was 'often seen in dancehalls and other public recreation spots', albeit that he was driven to such locales by his wife.[19]

Apart from attempting to curb KMT influence in the colony, Lao's emphasis under the direction of Zhou Enlai was on United Front work. This required influencing journalists, resident civil servants and business connections, as well as infiltration of moderate trade unions and non-government public relief agencies. The Chinese communists established their Hong Kong Central Branch Bureau back in 1947. James Tang contended that it was 'not set up to organise anti-Hong Kong government activities but to supervise and coordinate the Communist effort in their struggle against the Nationalists in South China and the South China Sea area'.[20]

The organisation of the CCP in Hong Kong thrived in the abundant commercial opportunities and their outlook on the British colony after 1945 was positive. Throughout the general calm of the early 1950s in Hong Kong, members of the KMT, just like the communists, were welcome in Hong Kong to stock up, buy and sell and make a profit. The CCP took full advantage of the protection given by colonial authorities to their political freedoms. One CIA report referred to openly held Communist Party meetings discussing 'the return to China of Hong Kong and Kowloon' at the Liu Kuo Hotel and in the office of newspaper *Hua Shang Pao* which were 'said to receive protection through the Office of Civil Affairs and the Police Department of the Hong Kong government'.[21] This liberality must factor positively in an assessment of the colonial anatomy.

The communists were most active in businesses of tobacco, recycling and commercial real estate. They did not, however, benefit from the indulgence and protection that some KMT figures enjoyed from colonial authorities. The local branch of the party had designated officers for intelligence, labour and union affairs, student affairs, materials inspection for imported goods, 'high intelligence' and 'subversion of Kuomintang agents and others'.[22] The British administration had offered the communist Chinese government consulate status, but Zhou Enlai rejected it because it implied the estrangement of Hong Kong from China.[23] This colonially enforced informality meant that the communist Chinese in Hong Kong operated through a network of trading officials with double lives in the Central Military Commission, the Bank of China or the Xinhua News Agency's so-called 'Security Department'.

In the two decades years after the Hong Kong Riot of 1956, Xinhua worked at coordinating the various entities into 'truly becoming a Communist front', as Cindy Chu put it.[24] Indeed, in this period the political officers of Xinhua outranked and outnumbered news-gathering reporters in the organisation, and Guangdong's municipal officials stepped aside from its supervisory role so that it was administered directly from the State Council's Foreign Affairs Office in Peking.[25] It has been thought that Zhou Enlai determined Hong Kong policy after running his thoughts past the Great Helmsman.

Not every CCP member undertook covert intelligence-gathering and political actions inside the colony. A senior member of Lao's Hong Kong set was Wu Ti-tsai, who was responsible for the communist labour unions and the major firm 'purchasing vital materials on behalf of the Communist Government'.[26] Chung Ta'tung was a communist agent in a similar line of work. He held an agency for the sale of tobacco on behalf of the communist government of China.[27] Hong Kong's role as the southern China depot for the communist rebuilding of the Chinese state after years of war was not discouraged by the British administration.

The Americans took careful note of communist investment in Hong Kong. Relying largely on bank contacts, physical surveillance and newspaper translations, they made life difficult for themselves by not participating in the Marco Polo Club, an informal monthly whiskey-sipping soiree the communist cadres used to exchange views and news with British officials and selected business leaders. CIA intelligence-gathering sought confirmed kills among the KMT raiding parties it funded to cross the Hong Kong border. Mainland newspapers were not the most reliable source.

There were occasions when the use of Hong Kong as an entrepot trade hub by the communists raised eyebrows in the CIA. In July 1950, HK$20 million in small denomination Hong Kong currency was deposited by the communists in several Hong Kong banks for the purchase of gasoline, cotton, rubber and metal casings suitable for bomb housings.[28] A report from early December 1950 stated the total amount to be HK$30 million, and the communist shopping list included a fleet of Dodge three-tonne trucks, purchased in Hong Kong and driven to Macau to pick up sixty-five cases of bomb casings and then forwarded to Canton, where a new airstrip was being built with cement from a British-owned cement company in Hong Kong, and fifty thousand spades purchased in Kowloon.[29] That was quite a sophisticated logistics effort. It highlighted the surprising degree of commercial freedom in the context of the Korean War offered to communist operatives in Hong Kong. It kept the colony quiet and generally uncontested in the early 1950s. It made the CIA restive.

Hong Kong became an indirect materials depot for the Chinese communist war effort in Korea, as well as for the suppression of reactionary elements still rattling around in southern China. The communists in Hong Kong were not above outright shadiness in their trade out of Hong Kong. In the guise of importing Western medicine and fifty refrigerators for hospitals in Tientsin, they engaged in what the CIA called 'secret ocean transportation' paying on one occasion HK$500,000 to a local shipowner for the use of a ship.[30] The colonial authorities apparently insisted that the ownership of the medical supplies company in charge of the transaction change from British to Chinese communist for the shipment to take place.[31]

In another transaction, a ship arrived in Hong Kong from Tientsin with Chinese medicine, silk and peanuts and departed to Tientsin with steel plate, iron bars and gunny sacks.[32] The Americans had a limited intelligence capability among the sailor and trading community extending to political and military issues on the coastal mainland. There were file references to communist ships from Tientsin unloading cargoes in Hong Kong of soybeans, bean cakes, pork and preserved eggs offered in exchange for construction materials and machinery, and 'one crew member reported there had been no interference from the Nationalists for the entire trip'.[33]

Another CIA report refers to several transactions by communist firms based in Canton purchasing hundreds of thousands of dollars in scrap metal, redundant airline equipment and a trading ship to sail from Hong Kong to Tientsin.[34] The account of the scrap metal transaction included a reference to it being: 'necessary to spend HK$10,000 for the bribes necessary to obtain an export license'.[35] The communists also owned a department store, banks, a trading company specialising in export of war materials, among other business and commercial endeavours.[36] Thus, there was a lively expenditure of money by the CCP in Hong Kong for a near-limitless variety of goods and services, including the provision of export licenses by corrupt British officials.

The same give and take of commercial permission in exchange for maintaining the political decorum of the colony applied in Hong Kong to communists and KMT representatives alike. If a serious political issue flared up, both would take to disruptive political actions. The pull of commercial tranquillity had a calming effect on many activists in most cases throughout the period between the end of the civil war in 1949 and the riot of 1956, except for a spate of political assassinations in 1951. Much of the British business-as-usual stance toward Korean War materials being sourced in Hong Kong dated from the late 1940s, when the Chinese were shipping phosphate fertiliser from North Korea via Norwegian freighters into Hong Kong for cash from South Americans in order to purchase goods necessary for the civil war with the KMT.[37] Members of the U.S. State Department were not happy about it, yet were aware that the British were generally discrete and that Hong Kong's free port status cut both ways.[38]

The communists in Hong Kong used business interests as a modus vivendi and as a mask for sinister actions, most notably detecting and arresting people fleeing their purges in southern China and assassinating high-value KMT targets in Hong Kong. One report from the CIA made reference to the Kwangtung Public Security Bureau's efforts to strengthen its position in Hong Kong. The report could have been describing an Ip Man movie when it referred to the Communist Party 'strengthening its assassination organisation in Hong Kong' by recruiting forty workers to train them in 'disguise, jumping from moving vehicles and the use of pistols'.[39] The communists were adept at espionage; they trained eighty individuals in Chienou who were formerly Nationalist government officials or military officers thought to have been packed off to subvert the KMT in Hong Kong.[40]

Examples of human rebirthing in Hong Kong and rival post-war legions living by their wits sounded unremarkable to those living inside the Hong Kong bubble. The report referred to communist agent Weng Lao, who was a member of the Kwangtung Public Security Bureau's border unit responsible for detecting KMT agents attempting to enter Kwangtung from Kowloon via Shenchuan. He was listed as formerly being a detective in the Police Department of the French Settlement in Shanghai, and 'a leader in the Shanghai underworld at one time'.[41] Long-faced or not, Weng's allegiance showed that communism expressed itself in a lightning strike, as well as congenital abnormality.

The distinction in business terms to be made by the British policy in Hong Kong toward the KMT and the communists might not seem so great. But thinking so would be a mistake. The British colonial government allowed the communists to use Hong Kong as an indirect supply depot and finance centre for the Korean War. But it stepped outside of a policy of mere communist and KMT equivalence in business freedom when it allowed the KMT to fund and train its militants to cross the border on suicide missions.

The political indifference of Hong Kong's financial institutions to whose money they took should not obscure, even after the Korean War had ended, their continuing regard for maintaining anatomical appearances of neutrality. Nor should the communist Chinese be assumed as their dupes. By the mid-1950s, they were prepared to call out the British KMT policy for what it was. They had been prepared to stay mute witnesses provided that, in the years from 1950 to 1954, British Hong Kong continued to absorb a king tide of abused and weary reactionaries from southern China who sought to make the colony their home, and Hong Kong could, at the same time, be used to help rebuild China.

After the 1956 riot, the communist appraisal of British colonialism became more refined than a list of demands. It became a critique aimed squarely at a characteristic of British colonialism often thought by its supporters to be a strength: the airy use of the rule of law as a pragmatic stand-in for human rights. In 1957 after the riot, a group of transport workers in a communist trade union sought to meet the Colonial Secretary but he refused to see them. Expecting such recalcitrance, they left a letter at his office. They observed frankly to the colonial government that after the riot 'despite our demands, the authorities did very little to punish the murderers and therefore many culprits are still at large'.[42]

The commutation of convicted murderer Chan Hon's death sentence to life in prison disappointed the workers making their post-riot testimony. Furthermore, these communists observed, 'the light sentences passed on or the acquittal of many other murderers would tend to make the Kuomintang agents think that they may still take another chance'.[43] This was observed by the communists in the post-civil war period when the British administration allowed the displaced KMT proxy Green and Red Pang criminal groups to infiltrate Hong Kong with refugees from central and northern China in the disguise of mutual aid societies.[44]

Communist trade unionists put the case in 1957 that another riot would occur in Hong Kong. They were not entirely wrong, albeit that the next major disturbance occurred in 1967 as the work of Chinese communists themselves. The riots of 1956 and 1967 book-ended an era of political turmoil in Hong Kong. The continued use of the colony throughout the late 1950s and the early 1960s as a base for KMT subterfuge and sabotage raids on the mainland was made possible by the soft response of the colonial administration to KMT and pro-KMT gangster crimes given example in the first riot. The most desperate fringe of the culprits and enablers of 1956 formed the gene pool drawn on by Taipei to commit terrorist outrages in southern China throughout the late 1950s.

Ignoring assassins

Hong Kong's non-enforcement of criminal law in contexts of political violence characterised the British response to the riot of 1956. It dated from an earlier time. In one CIA anecdote, the Hong Kong scene was so in the vein of cloak and dagger in 1951 that a senior KMT general was assassinated in his favourite restaurant, which he had no idea was owned and operated by the communists.[45] When there occurred a spate of symbolic killing by both extremes of politics in that year, they could be thought to be continuing to enact the civil war in Hong Kong. However, the British colonial administration usually turned a blind eye to tit-for-tat political killings because they did not threaten public order in a manner that seriously questioned British sovereignty in Hong Kong. The British administration's position, then, was that the KMT could use the colony as a safe house, but that if it turned out not to be that safe, it would not prosecute communist assassins.

The CIA named Lo Yao-ch'ang as 'chief of communist terrorist activities in Hong Kong with the mission of assassination Nationalist figures there', along with Liang Hsieh and Liang Yun-ching as members of a communist assassination group.[46] Although at large, such men were themselves figures in the sights of KMT agents. As we will note in the immediate aftermath of the 1956 riot, there was a notable technique of British colonialism in Hong Kong not to bring attention to their criminal justice response to political violence with high-profile prosecutions if the triadic commercial order remained intact after the death or handed the communists an avoidable martyrdom.

Going in softly against the KMT agents in the 1956 riot and selecting small-time racketeers, bystanders or non-politicals instead for prosecution, as well as playing a straight bat to communist compensation claims, formed the default position of the British administration accustomed to following KMT money as a mode of justice. It had the added benefit of appeasing the U.S. State Department which continued to support KMT remnants as freedom fighters. The British officials of Hong Kong noticed how the communists sounded monotonous when they complained. The issue of light punishment for KMT agents was one the communists would not easily forget.

The anti-rightist purges in mainland China

KMT and communist opportunism in the fields of business and espionage in early 1950s Hong Kong occurred in a context of extreme political instability in southern China in the wake of the civil war. The war had officially ended. What remained of the KMT's military and civil leadership had fled to Taiwan and Hong Kong. An assortment of KMT guerrillas and KMT-aligned warlords commanded forces well into thousands of men who fought sporadic battles with the People's Liberation Army (PLA) for territorial control in pockets of the southern provinces, and elsewhere throughout China.

Some of Hong Kong's wealthiest Chinese businessmen held on to their British allegiances tightly after the civil war. Others backed KMT militants, along with the Americans. Yet others still put money into non-aligned guerrilla forces who gave hope to eventually winning back their sponsors' residential and industrial property across the border. The larger context of anti-nationalist purging magnified the importance of Hong Kong as a site of resistance. It demanded the British colonial administration develop a strategy that optimised the labour and investment input of refugee KMT elements who did not wave the nationalist flag too vigorously on Hong Kong soil. The KMT resistance in the Canton area in China and communist truth-telling in Hong Kong offer a counterpoint to each other ignored in the historiography, despite occurring only a few hundred kilometres apart.

The ultimate British policy in Hong Kong would be to eliminate units of the KMT continuing to advance military aspirations in China from Hong Kong. In 1950, that position was more than a decade away. The British colonial government figures not only turned a blind eye to KMT resistance. They ignored the Maoist horrors unfolding in mainland China, but could not ignore the refugees it generated. The Rightist exodus from the hostile conditions of the mainland became a key element in the colony's post-war success. They slipped into the colony as construction labourers. This flood of scared humanity contained in it the rioters of 1956 and the bomb-makers arrested in 1963. The mixed blessing of migration from communist-era China was a slow enlightenment for the British authorities in Hong Kong.

Only by understanding the adverse conditions encountered by KMT civil and military leaders after 1949 can Hong Kong as a destination for commercial opportunists, armed militants and corrupt old regime officials stripe make sense. The civil war, along with the resistance that continued after it, modified neither the anatomies nor the underlying practice of the KMT or the CCP. During the mid-Autumn festival of 1950, the CCP called on ex-KMT soldiers in a refugee camp in Rennie's Mill, East Kowloon to repent their errant ways. It sent them a written message along such lines. It referred to the ex-soldiers as 'stateless and pitiful creatures' who were 'slaves of imperialists and tools of American brigands'. [47] It warned the soldiers that they were 'enemies of their own people' who had been 'duped by illusory dreams' and that the mainland government would be 'generous to you all'. [48] It concluded:

> Hong Kong is no paradise, for Hong Kong is also one of our objectives. Where, then, will you go? The British imperialists will not always be able to protect you. [49]

This was a scare tactic. Possessing Hong Kong was not a communist objective. The message offered a chance to the soldiers to 'turn your thoughts to your home country, repent and serve your own people'.[50] Yet no second chance awaited those who returned to China. There should be no attempt to gloss over the mistruths and state terror enlisted by the Chinese communists to consolidate their grasp on China after 1949. Chapter 4 will refer to the Autumn festival message as an example of the impossibly complex anatomical position the CCP constructed for itself in the eyes of expatriate Chinese.

The slaughter

Soon after the invasion of southern Korea by the Chinese communist-backed 'People's Army', Mao Tse-tung announced a purge of Rightists in his own country. It formed part of the CCP obsession for purity in leadership brought by elimination of reactionary supporter bases. It took a breathtaking toll on what was left of the KMT. Premier Zhou Enlai did not shy away from a figure of one million saboteurs and guerrillas slain by communist forces in the twenty-one months after the end of the civil war.[51] Another report in 1951 offered a view that, 'by the admission of the communists themselves', one and a half million anti-communists had been purged and that several more innocents had been caught up in the systematic elimination of Old Society and active counter-revolutionary elements.[52]

The purge included dissident intellectuals and artists, the so-called 'man-eating' landlords and fishing despots, senior Chinese employees of the now-defunct foreign factory and banking systems, KMT military and civilian personnel as well.[53] It was a frontal attack on old order bourgeoisie who had clung on rather than flee. The day the purge was announced? None other than the Double Ten Holiday, 10 October 1950. Traditionally a day of nationalist celebration to mark the establishment of the first republic in 1912, there could be no mistaking the date's significance. Mao's program of retribution had been in full swing since April 1950, using Chungking and Shanghai as its trial sites. After the Double Ten, it rolled out nationally.

The homicidal chaos of the Cultural Revolution takes much of the historical attention away from the firing squads and shallow graves of 1950–1951. Intelligence officers of the Kuomintang claimed that the CCP plan was to eliminate five hundred people in each of 2,087 districts they had created to divide up China; plus at least a thousand people in each of sixty-seven medium-sized towns and about five thousand in each of the twelve biggest cities.[54] This would come to a total of around one million people; many believed it was closer to double that by the end of 1951.[55] The widened bounds of CCP membership converged with a policy of eliminating unaffiliated old regime supporters to determine the fate of millions. The purge devoured innocents to deter a slip backward to a market economy under a skin of progressive constitutionalism.

Little reflection is given to the nature of China's innocents. The arbitrariness of daily life under early communist rule was a frequent cause for comment in the liberal media outside the country: 'anyone found uncooperative in the slightest manner can be arrested and shot at any moment in any locality',[56] maintained one expatriate dissident, and not without cause. For each village work group after 1950, an extra 5 percent loading on the reactionary quota was added for trial and execution to include people who might have been KMT or not. Some can only regard this as callous. Coloured by a dreading paranoia, the policy nevertheless underestimated the millions who had played survival games by flip-flopping their political identity in the last years of the civil war. They were neither communists nor able after Liberation to contrive enthusiasm for New China much above resigned acceptance.

Mao Tse-tung had ultimately rejected Stalin's advice to form a national reconciliation government with the KMT. Decisive to his enemies, he chose a high road for his genus of communism. It was possible because CCP and PLA membership had been porous between 1945 and 1949. Although a high road had been chosen, its paving remained undecided. Under the leadership of Mao Tse-tung, Li Shaoqi, Zhou Enlai, Zhu De, Chen Yun and Lin Biao, a troubling policy tension emerged. China agonised between the peasant principle of Yen'an rectification to maintain Red 'peasant' thinking and the urban technological advancement thought necessary to elevate the Chinese masses to their own modernity.[57] As resisting or not resisting the CCP lead to the same fate, a widely demoralised society lived through uncertain days. A people without choice was ruled by the whims of a handful of zealots. Too often, this state of affairs underlay the communist anatomy claiming to rule for 'the people'.

Anti-Rightist purge quotas remained in place after the initial years of CCP consolidation.[58] The purge fed on bystanders as well as carefully identified political targets. Among the southern China provinces, the landlords of Hunan suffered particular scrutiny. They were:

> outstandingly recalcitrant to the land reform program [as they] continue to sabotage it in many ways, destroying buildings, groves, and farm animals and equipment, and assassinating land-reform cadres.[59]

If a landlord vanished, one was presumed to have joined reactionary bandits in the hills, or more likely, had spirited away grain and equipment to another province. Such landlords were regarded as cowards for leaving family members remaining in the village to face the music for their resistance or intransigence. Before long, there was nowhere left to run for the landlords of Hunan. Canton's communist press went out of its way to put a black mark on southern landlords. It raised an anatomy contrasting revolutionary contributors with leaches from the old regime. One editorial identified organised resistance after a sabotage raid: 'the bandits were assisted by the unscrupulous reactionary landlords in their activities'.[60]

A landlord who took their prescribed ideological medicine, participated in re-education, and was unproblematic for five years, could re-join the working class as a labourer but, 'no landlord will be permitted to live the parasitical existence heretofore'.[61] Life in China became dire for Kuomintang adherents and their coattails. One trade union delegate who escaped the madness by making it to Hong Kong said that most people in China preferred the civil war to living in a country under Russian control – a widely held view of Mao's collectivist and industrial planning regime among Taiwan-based KMT ranks.[62]

Being too closely associated with private property ownership lead to being killed or banished in China after the civil war. The communist neurosis over counter-revolution permeated the countryside as well as the towns:

> landlords connived with KMT special agents to assassinate cadres and progressive peasants and created disorder by arousing rabble and backward peasants to attack cadres. In some places, they stirred up strife between villages, which led to bloodshed, in order to break down the unity of the masses.[63]

When one finds oneself on the losing side after a civil war, the options are limited. Anti-communist resistance in the hills offered a principled way out for people who had not taken it through suicide or fled with a gangster cache to Hong Kong or Taiwan.

Migration surges to Hong Kong in 1957 and 1961 resulted from the politically arbitrary and anti-capitalist environment of early communist China. What Lifton giddily described as the communist 'heaven-storming heroic effort and . . . austerity'[64] displaced the pre-1949 triad cosmopolitan economy of monopolism enforced by street violence. This shift forced unprecedented numbers of gangsters to relocate, as well as villagers exhausted by living in fear. A surge of people crossed over the border to Hong Kong, where they were generally accepted as cheap labour by the diffident British authorities. It turned out that the gangsters were not much good at retraining.

The conditions in China in the early 1950s created conditions of Hong Kong's political liberality which, in turn, made it a base for KMT counter-measures conducted in mainland China throughout the decade. Militant elements of the KMT in Hong Kong persisted on a throaty elixir of cross-border identity fraud, protection racket fundraising, arms smuggling, espionage training and a thriving market in bolt-hole real estate. Occasional flexes of terrorist muscle on the mainland showed sufficiently diminishing returns only when the 1960s dawned.

KMT resistance activities

The communists won the civil war. They also had to win the peace in a country that had become a shambles of factions. The KMT had large military forces in southern China after 1949 still capable of fighting. However, the historical claims about early communist China do not always tally. Communist sources estimated that, from the 1,400,000 KMT guerrillas who had been active in China, one million had been 'annihilated'.[65] Western estimates presented a more optimistic picture: 1.2 million KMT guerrillas had been reinforced to 1.8 million, and 60 percent were armed, giving them 'sufficient strength to cause Communist forces a great deal of difficulty'.[66]

In 1950, communism in southern China could be a thin or thick rice gruel depending on where one dined. From Western Hunan to Kwangtung there were hundreds of thousands of KMT guerrillas engaging in harassing actions and outright attacks on communist forces throughout 1950. There were mass defections from the KMT to the communists. Other KMT soldiers made for home during harvest times and maintained an active guerrilla career at other times. Some were under control of warlords with no political agenda except opportunistic pillage. Yet other KMT elements formed part of the border-fringing anti-communist armies armed and officered directly by Taiwan.

Despite CCP claims to the contrary, there was nothing pragmatic or forward-looking about the anti-Rightist military response. The Chinese state media claimed in 1950 that the activities of KMT saboteurs 'required extreme precautions to protect our economy' because they 'plundered granaries, disrupt communications, produce counterfeit notes to make the currency unstable etc'.[67] It reported the arrest of Mao Sen the 'Chief of KMT special agents' in Qingdao who was directing the Shandong People's Anti-communist National Salvation Army which was reportedly 'well supplied with explosives'.[68] The report also cited cases of a rubber worker spoiling a batch of rubber resulting in 860,000 shoes being made useless and various acts of sabotage to machines and cloth, stealing parts, cutting power lines, posing as police to obtain transport plans and stealing economic information, 'often done with connivance of the people's government'.[69]

Despite such episodes of strategic truth-telling, and examples of old-fashioned industrial incompetence dressed up as the acts of a fiendish sleeper cell, China had a counter-revolution on its hands. The nation found itself mired in a national identity problem in the years following the civil war not necessarily alleviated by eliminating the KMT as a rival government. Elsewhere, there were echoes of bourgeois culture and governance that the communists themselves admitted were slippery opponents responsive only to banishment.

After the outbreak of the Korean conflict, several KMT guerrilla units were strengthened by the defection of former communist troops in the Tung Chiang area of Kwangtung who believed a rumour that Taiwan nationalist forces were preparing to attack mainland China.[70] The Hong Kong-based Rightist newspaper *Kung-shang Jih-pao* (*KSJP*) reported that a visitor to the colony gave word that Hunan guerrillas known as the Anti-Communist National Salvation Army had been putting up posters in public places about its position on the Korean War and MacArthur's trip to Taiwan and that 'as a result of being more enlightened on current events, the masses are forming anti-Communist feelings'.[71] The communists had to take seriously these threats to its control of a unified China.

The year of 1950 was a difficult one for communist forces trying to assert total control over China's southern provinces. An outbreak of guerrilla violence by 40,000 KMT 'remnants' in Sikiang (South of Guangzhou) in February 1950 was reported gleefully in *KSJP* to be 'causing great distress to the communist authorities'.[72] The unease of the communists as they advanced southward to reinforce their takeover of Canton and the southwest border regions led them to warn local populations that KMT special agents were operating in large numbers in their areas. They were said to be 'infiltrating Kwangtung from Hong Kong and Macau' and 'actively soliciting the support of local bandits to organise the so-called "Kwangtung Anti-communist Liberation Army Assault Unit"'.[73]

KSJP also reported on August 1950 that 'after the outbreak of the Korean conflict, a rumour that Taiwan nationalist forces were preparing to attack the mainland caused many guerrillas in the Tzu-chin and Wu-ha area [east of Guangzhou in Guangdong province] to rise up actively against the communist forces'.[74] It was further reported that seven hundred communist troops had attacked the KMT diehards in these areas and 150 communist fighters were injured or killed in the attempt to suppress them.[75]

Unchecked movement of KMT agents across the Hong Kong border became such a concern of the communist Chinese after 1956 that they raised it repeatedly with the British colonial administration. British officials quite cleverly characterised Hong Kong's open port status as holding an all-or-nothing character as if, when pushed, it would banish from the colony everyone with a political opinion. War-related materials of the United States and communist China were freely procured by payment into Hong Kong bank accounts. Both countries tested the British by being churlish on their policies toward the KMT. The British diplomatic recognition of China, while simultaneously maintaining all sorts of remnant KMT relationships, underlined that British foreign policy rarely clarified its ambiguity unless absolutely forced to by events. This united the refugee Cantonese middle class of Hong Kong and mainland communists in a shared opinion. The long-standing presumption of the British to play the game and adjudicate it at the same time could come as no surprise to any seasoned observer of Hong Kong.

By 1953, the communist struggle for control over southern China was over. Mopping up survivors into concentration camps in Szechuan province replaced administration of systematic roving parties hunting down counter-revolutionary bandits. At the provincial, county and village levels, the communist regime held in prison approximately two million people from the old landlord and merchant classes as well as KMT military figures, political officials and their affiliates in the Young China Party and the Democratic Socialists.[76] The prisoners were put to work on dam building, road construction, irrigation projects and ground levelling for building construction.

Those set to guard over those who had survived the purge were notoriously brutal. One anecdote concerned the fate of Li Po-shen, a Shanghai lawyer who had been Sun Yat-sen's secretary, as well as Secretary General of Szechuan province under the Nationalist government, and Nationalist China's first Chief Justice. As a communist prisoner, one day he fell too ill to eat rice, and when he sought rice water instead, was severely beaten by the guards and died later that evening in his cell.[77]

China has been cursed by the kind of social tragedy not necessarily understood better by explaining it. The lack of sympathy demonstrated by the communists fills the pages of Dikötter and Yang Jisheng. Yet revisiting the catalogue of horrors offers no post-genocidal catharsis. The communists were paranoid, but not entirely delusional. If they believed it inevitable that the KMT's resistance would be crushed, the genie did stand a chance of escaping from the bottle again. The civil war had not been about a couple of bourgeois options struggling to reach ascendancy under a foreign paymaster. Those were the days of Yuan Shikai playing at independence. Nor was it a proto-proletarian revolt against a feudal monarchy propped up by Westerners, as the Taiping episode had been. It was about making China and its tens of millions of rural peasants into a country with its own economy and foreign policy.

Li Po-shen sadly shared the same lamentable fate as millions of people with or without political cause to be punished by the communist regime as it anchored itself in power in the early 1950s. It was certainly unlawful in liberal human rights terms. Yet its purpose as a slate-cleaning exercise – paranoid, purity-crazed and devoid of dignity – cannot be called a historical nullity.

Conclusion

The communist anatomy found itself greatly overextended compared to the colonial one. Its cringing recognition politics, plus a craving for a stable and capitalist Hong Kong, were at odds with its anti-colonial anatomy. The flaws of communist anatomy were exposed by its anti-capitalist purging of the KMT in southern China 1950–1951, and its toleration of Hong Kong's use as a KMT remnant base for resistance raids in the southern hinterland. As for the communists, one of their senior diplomats in Shanghai in 1956 pointed out to his counterpart, in English, that: 'you know we could cause plenty of trouble in Hong Kong easily, but we don't want to'.[78]

Resistance to colonialism, and anti-capitalism, were prominent in the anatomy of communist China. In the frenzied reckoning grounds of mainland China in 1950–1951, having foreign acquaintances or a stubborn capitalist in the family was enough to get one summarily executed. Comparing the anatomy with the mainland reality made Hong Kong a site of communist contradiction. Muted recognition of colonialism and co-existence with it ruled most of the 1950s. This meant that the communists would have to accept the 1956 riot blame as the rough, if they were to remain in Hong Kong, along with the smooth of commercial access. The CCP was either pro-capitalist or anti-capitalist, depending on which bit of southern China one cared to look. Treating Hong Kong as a special case did not put the CCP in a principled position to argue with the imperialists, much less 'destroy the headquarters of imperialism and reaction' as one of their propaganda films put it.[79]

The KMT did not go quietly, but raised bedlam instead. The party put up a spirited fight against overwhelming odds in southern China for a decade after the civil war ended. The anti-Rightist purges came in steady waves, crashing to shore hard due to the CCP's lack of self-assurance. The resistance of the KMT, and the support of the British, split the anatomy of communism in southern China. Communism conceded to capitalism for a while.

Among its own, the CCP's favourite methodology attacked indifference as the cause of social isolationism and disharmony. Cadres asked closed questions in the guise of open inquiry into an individual's habits and morals. Struggle sessions were aggressive and manipulative to a high order, as were the various amnesties of thought and residence. The energy expended in a communist system in maintaining its anatomy was considerably higher than that required by a colonial system. When the communists were in a colonial system, their normal means of creating and maintaining their anatomy were ineffectual. Although its offer to the masses to learn precepts of modernity could be transformative in a way that no colonial anatomy would dare to suggest possible, it was liable to confused goal messaging in the absence of a hometown crowd.

When riots broke out in Hong Kong on 10 October 1956, they must have seemed to the leadership of the CCP a gift from heaven. Hong Kong could be added to Egypt as an example of the faltering judgments in British colonialism in that year, and distract attention from the increasingly fervent implementation of communist reforms in Tibet. The riots were a perfect opportunity to question the credibility of a vestige of colonialism on China's southern shore. The whole firmament of Chinese communism depended not only on the confidence of its strides but on the opportunities capitalist enemies offered when they faltered. What was the reality of life in Hong Kong, and what was used by the communists to discredit colonial ideology?

Did the Chinese Communist Party fully capitalise on the riot in Hong Kong in October 1956? Did the riot align the communist anatomy with a plausible orthodoxy in southern China? Did the communist anatomy lay eclipsed by the colonial anatomy after 1956? The use of legality to achieve a political purpose by colonial authorities in 1956 injured their anatomy, if not fatally. This did not prevent the growing assertiveness of the communist anatomy in the years after 1956 or its plausible alignment a reality in public sentiment.

Notes

1 HKRS 184-4-21: 'Kuomintang Activities': 'Telegram: Government House HK: A. Grantham to HBM Embassy Nanking' 24 June 1948 (6/7761/ 1948), [13].
2 Mark Chi-kwan, *The Everyday Cold War: Britain and China 1950–1972* (London: Bloomsbury, 2017), 22.
3 Lois Michison, 'Hong Kong Riots', *New Statesman and Nation* (20 October 1956), 5.
4 Michison, 5.
5 Christine Loh, *Underground Front: The Chinese Communist Party in Hong Kong* (Hong Kong: Hong Kong University Press, 2010), 87.
6 Anne Freemantle (ed), *Mao Tse-tung: An Anthology of His Writings* (New York: Mentor, 1962), 290–291.
7 Loh, 69.
8 Presumably this refers to U.S. Marines stationed in Qingdao at the request of the KMT in the wake of the Japanese withdrawal.

9 CIA-RDP82-00457R000300360008-5: 'Political Information: Communists in Hong Kong' (4 January 1947), 1.
10 HKMS 158-3-1, 'Telegram 1: O'Neil, Peking to FO' (16 October 1956), [5].
11 HKRS 163-1-2029 (523/57/58): 'Communist Accounts': 'Workers Protest Against Riot Compensation' (clippings from *Ta Kung Pao* 31 August 1957).
12 Anthony Brown, 'The Societies Specialise in Violence' *The Canberra Times* (7 August 1964), 2.
13 HKMS 158-3-1, 'Telegram 1', [4].
14 CIA-RDP82-00457R002800260006-1: 'Movement of Chinese Communists and Sympathizers From Hong Kong to Communist Controlled Areas' (6 June 1949), 1.
15 CIA-RDP82-00457R002800260006-1: 'Movement of Chinese Communists', 1.
16 CIA-RDP82-00457R006200670004-0: '1. Chinese Communist Intentions Toward Hong Kong 2. Chinese Military Activity in Kwuntung Province' (9 November 1950), 1.
17 CIA-RDP82-00457R008900210011-3: 'Activities of Chinese Communists in Hong Kong', (23 October 1951) 1–2.
18 CIA-RDP82-00457R008900210011-3: 'Activities of Chinese Communists', 2.
19 CIA-RDP82–00457R008900210011–3: 'Activities of Chinese Communists', 2.
20 James Tang, 'World War to Cold War: Hong Kong's Future and Anglo-Chinese Interactions, 1941–55' in Ming Chan (ed), *Precarious Balance Hong Kong Between China and Britain 1842–1992* (Hong Kong: Hong Kong University Press, 1994), 116.
21 CIA-RDP82-00457R000300360008-5: 'Political Information: Communists in Hong Kong', 1.
22 CIA-RDP82-00457R008900210011-3: 'Activities of Chinese Communists in Hong Kong', 2.
23 Loh, 81.
24 Cindy Chu, *Chinese Communists and Hong Kong Capitalists 1937–1997* (New York: Palgrave Macmillan, 2010), 47.
25 Chu, 47.
26 CIA-RDP82-00457R008900210011-3: 'Activities of Chinese Communists', 2.
27 CIA-RDP82–00457R008900210011–3: 'Activities of Chinese Communists', 1.
28 CIA-RDP82-00457R005500290006-8: '1. Hong Kong Currency. 2. Chinese Communist Purchases, Hong Kong' (8 August 1950), [2].
29 CIA-RDP82-00457R006500420012-8: '1. Chinese Communist Purchases in Hong Kong 2. Shipments from Hong Kong to Chinese Mainland' (13 December 1950), [1]-[5].
30 CIA-RDP80-00810A002600990007-8: '1. Fuel Oil Supplies, Communist China 2. Shipment of Refrigerators 3. J.K. Willy and Co, Hong Kong' (22 October 1953), [1].
31 CIA-RDP80-00810A002600990007-8: '1. Fuel Oil Supplies', [1].

32 CIA-RDP82-00457R005400680009-3: '1. OMSNC Ships in Hong Kong 2. Communist Shipment From Hong Kong to Tientsin' (7 August 1950), [4].

33 CIA-RDP80-00809A000600360969-7: 'Communists Step up Shipping Service to Hong Kong 2. Foreign Ships Continue to Call Communist Ports' (18 December 1950), [1]-[2].

34 CIA-RDP82-00457R006700210007-2: '1. Chinese Communist Commercial Activities and Firms', 2. From Hong Kong and Macau' (19 January 1951), [2].

35 CIA-RDP82-00457R006700210007-2: '1. Chinese Communist Commercial Activities', 1.

36 CIA-RDP82-00457R006700210007-2: '1. Chinese Communist Commercial Activities', 1.

37 CIA-RDP82-00457R006700210007-2: '1. Chinese Communist Commercial Activities', 1.

38 CIA-RDP82-00457R002300400004-2: '1. Economic Information: Chinese Communist Procurement Activities in Hong Kong . . .' (10 February 1949), [2].

39 CIA-RDP82-00457R008000290002-4: 'Chinese Communist Terrorist Activities in the Hong Kong/Kowloon Area' (17 August 1951), 1.

40 CIA-RDP82-00457R008000290002-4: 'Chinese Communist Terrorist Activities', 1.

41 CIA-RDP82-00457R008000290002-4: 'Chinese Communist Terrorist Activities', 2.

42 HKRS 163-1-2029; 526/57/58: 'Communist Accounts'.

43 HKRS 163-1-2029; 526/57/58: 'Communist Accounts'.

44 K. Bolton and K. Hutton, *Triad Societies: Triad Societies in Hong Kong* (London: Taylor & Francis, 2002), 59–80.

45 CIA-RDP82-00457R008000290002-4: 'Chinese Communist Terrorist Activities', 1.

46 CIA-RDP82-00457R008000290002-4: 'Chinese Communist Terrorist Activities', 1.

47 CIA-RDP82-00457R006200710001-8: 'Chinese Communist Message to Refugees in Hong Kong' (15 November 1950), 1.

48 CIA-RDP82-00457R006200710001-8: 'Chinese Communist Message', 1.

49 CIA-RDP82-00457R006200710001-8: 'Chinese Communist Message', 1.

50 CIA-RDP82-00457R006200710001-8: 'Chinese Communist Message', 1.

51 Robert Shaplen, 'Guerrillas – Our Hope in Red China' *Collier's* (21 July 1951), 13.

52 Leon Dennen, "Eyewitness Report: 'Frightful Reign of Terror' in Red China" *New York World – Telegram and Sun* (28 July 1951), 15.

53 Shaplen, 15.

54 Shaplen, 13.

55 Shaplen, 13.

56 Dennen, 15.

57 Jean Chesneaux, *Peasant Revolts in China 1840–1949* (London: Thames Hudson, 1973), 165.

58 Bill Brugger, *China: Liberation and Transformation 1942–1962* (London: Croom Helm, 1981), 91.

59 CIA-RDP80-00809A000600380626-5: 'Economic. Agriculture, Land Reform' translated excerpts from communist newspapers (30 March 1951), 1.

60 CIA-RPD80-00809A000600320264-3, 'CCF Reports KMT Guerrilla Units Killed or Captured in Recent Campaigns': 'Kwangsi Bandits Wiped Out' (Canton *Nan Fang Jih-pao*) (17 April 1950), 1.

61 CIA-RDP80-00809A000600380626-5: 'Economic. Agriculture, Land Reform', 1.

62 Dennen, 15.

63 CIA-RDP80-00809A000600380626-5: 'Economic. Agriculture, Land Reform', 2.

64 Robert Jay Lifton, *Revolutionary Immortality: Mao Tse-tung and the Chinese Cultural Revolution* (Weidenfeld: London, 1968), 82–83.

65 CIA-RDP80-00809A000600350504-3: 'KMT Guerrilla Activities Continue in Various Localities' (18 October 1950), 1.

66 CIA-RDP80-00809A000600350504-3: 'KMT Guerilla Activities Continue', 1.

67 CIA-RDP80-00809A000600340704-2, 'KMT Agents Continue Sabotage' (17 July 1950), 1.

68 CIA-RDP80-00809A000600350504-3: 'KMT Guerrilla Activities Continue', 1.

69 CIA-RDP80-00809A000600350504-3: 'KMT Guerrilla Activities Continue', 1.

70 CIA-RDP80-00809A000600350504-3, 'KMT Guerrilla Activities Continue', 2.

71 CIA-RDP80-00809A000600350504-3, 'KMT Guerrilla Activities Continue', 2.

72 CIA-RDP80-00809A000600300078-2, 'KMT Guerrillas Harass Southern Areas; Communists Arrest KMT agents in Peiping, Fu-Chou' (11 April 1950), 2.

73 CIA-RDP80-00809A000600300662-3: 'KMT Guerrilla Attacks Increase in Kwangtung; CCF Warns Against KMT Agents' (2 May 1950), 1.

74 CIA-RDP80-00809A000600350504-3: 'KMT Guerrilla Activities Continue', 1.

75 CIA-RDP80-00809A000600350504-3: 'KMT Guerrilla Activities Continue', 1.

76 CIA-RDP80-00810A001400600003-7: 'Chinese Communist Concentration Camps, Szechuan' (18 June 1953), 1.

77 CIA-RDP80-00810A001400600003-7: 'Chinese Communist Concentration Camps', 2.

78 HKMS 158-3-1: 'Telegram 1: O'Neil, Peking to FO' (16 October 1956), [10].

79 CCP, *The East Is Red: Chinese Song and Dance Epic* (Motion picture, 1965).

2 The colonial anatomy
The 1956 riot

Introduction

The previous chapter found that the KMT fought a hopeless war of resistance against the CCP for control of southern China in 1950–1951, continuing with outbursts of violence well into the 1960s. During this time, the anti-capitalist anatomy of the communists on full display on the mainland was muffled in Hong Kong due to its sorely needed commercial stability. The significance of the riots in Hong Kong of 1956 lay not in their cause, or the human suffering or property damage they were responsible for, although all these were substantial. What mattered to history was way that their biased political interpretation in colonial eyes intensified communist critique of British rule in Hong Kong. The riots could be considered resistance, either as an episode of KMT attention-seeking over the shanty-town depravity of the colony or an ad hoc but unsuccessful provocation of communists in the colony. Either way, the riots provoked two unanswered communist questions:

1 Why was Hong Kong colonial if its ruling foreign power could not guarantee good order?
2 Why did KMT militants and street toughs have a free hand in Hong Kong?

The communists' questions about the riot signalled re-emergence of their visibly anti-colonial anatomy in the colony, but not a conciliatory realignment of the colonial anatomy in light of communist grievance. The questions of the communists suggested disturbing anomalies underneath the colonial anatomy. The anatomy of colonial Hong Kong advertised an idea that a balance was maintained by giving everyone something. The riot called that into question.

Imagine the scene. A late morning rumble and pop of fireworks in Kowloon signalled the celebration of the Double Ten Holiday of 1956. The lion dancers donned their costume and started their warm-up gymnastics. Scooping up and down alleyways in kites of colour, their symmetry and coordination were something to behold. The ritual of going from door to door with the lion offering its blessing to businesses in exchange for a small fee could suggest an offer of mafia protection, or an innocent communal hope for seasonal providence. The Double Ten holiday was disparaged by the British and the communists alike because of the fresh enmities it could stir up. By the mid-1950s, an article of faith among the exiled KMT conclaves in Taiwan and Hong Kong was that if one could not make merry about recent history, one could always make trouble.

In 1950s Hong Kong, an excess of rice wine and a dispute in a wet market over fish bought on credit could put some sort of crazy-making with meat cleavers in prospect. An argumentative air hung over Hong Kong on 10 October 1956. An official from the Refugee Reception Centre in Shamshui Po reportedly strolled out and yanked down a poster repeating nationalist slogans. In a crazy arrhythmia of drum beats, the lion took to its rampage. Lumps of concrete rained down on the roof of the makeshift reception centre. Doors were locked. Chairs came in through the windows. People would pay for declining the lion's protection.

The holiday had begun. The riot lashed out everywhere. Its victims included perpetrators and bystanders. Mr Leung Tong had worked for five years in Ngai Wah Clothing's factory outlet in Sham Shui Po, Kowloon as a ladies' garment salesman. On Friday 12 October 1956, he fell ill at work after taking his lunch. Deciding to walk home and to rest in the afternoon, Leung made his way along Yuen Chau Street and approached its junction with Cheung Sha Wan Road at 2:30 p.m. Discovering a civil disturbance there, on his widow's account, he was struck and fatally injured by a tear gas shell deployed by soldiers occupying the junction.

He died in a police cell in Sham Shui Po Police Station later that night.

The compensation case brought by Leung Tong's wife, Mrs Ho Mo Ching[1] could be given any one of many interpretations. Her view of an innocent man caught up in events beyond his reckoning was not accepted by the police or the compensation board. She sought a small payment for losing her husband and thus her family's livelihood. Her claim was refused.

Not much is gained by analysing a riot. In the beginning, it is about unguarded shops and petty feuds or chance encounters made brutal by the absence of restraint. No-one calculates consequence. One person or another threw a brick into a window and snatched a radio. Some toughs overturned a car and murdered its terrified passenger; others stormed a post-office and emptied the tills. A riot peaks and fails like a gyroscope in its last throes. A curfew is not a presumption of guilt to people always thought guilty. So it begins to spin again after dark.

Who started or egged on the riot of 1956 is a much less important question than the policy response colonial authorities gave to riotous behaviour. What it said about the political imbalance normal to the colony and whether or not justice was done to Mr Leung and his widow could be totemic. Being a family man and a stable employee might not prevent him becoming an opportunist in the heat of a riot – in Cobb's description, the wine merchant had become an uncouth riverside worker.[2] Yet the lack of serious investigation in Leung's case, and the unanswered questions it raised, suggests indifference to truth or a tight control on plausibility among colonial authorities. The political purpose of government indifference will be explained in this chapter as a reality of late British colonialism beneath its apparently compensative anatomy.

Let the question of who started the riot be asked as if it is important to give it an answer. Then we can reflect on Leung Tong's compensation case from all sides to consider what it reveals about the anatomy of a riot. No citizen was permitted neutrality by colonialism when pressure was put on its anatomical claim to offer due process. Compelling ordinary people to continue to subscribe to colonialism when they had experienced the opposite of fair dealing made future enemies out of them. But this did not really matter when the disappointed people were not important. Opportunists and clueless people just trying to get home could be the most suitable targets of blame compared to rioters more intimately connected to colonial authority. It was a bonus if the collaterals were dead.

Various modes of anatomy exist in submerged forms of ideology to this day. Visible in the old colonies as a defensive tendency to defend historical hierarchy, and its allocations, or in the way a state decides its usurpers by arraying incontrovertible positions that have no history, or presents a history that is more like redaction than proposition, every anatomy avoids questions that would make its private purpose public. It worked without noise in the glare and gloom of collective perception to make an explanation. Not a call to action, but a plausible line to agree with, each colonial administration took great care to superintend its anatomy in the case of a riot. How it occurred, and who was to blame, were questions with answers elevated to the highest heights of public record, even if the question of why those compensated had been deemed deserving seemed oddly unanswered by the compensation exercise itself.

The anatomy of a riot was the anatomy of a colony. Every element of it was distorted to some degree. A colonial administration always ended a riot by calling in the troops at exactly the right moment, and minor riot criminality, such as breach of curfew, was usually the most widely punished. During the aftermath of a colonial riot, no administrator in their right mind would draw attention to social conditions in the colony as a reason for the riot. That was not done.

The nihilistic resistance of the KMT in Hong Kong and southern China (1950–1962) was recognised by the British administration, if not the KMT itself, and this allowed British administrators to manage its importance for over a decade. Although the KMT's violent resistance was spontaneous, and without any hope of securing a sentimental return to its past, it was not obscure or risible. This state of affairs highlighted the maladjusted nature of the British in their continuing colonialism.

By refraining from a condemnation of post-1949 KMT counter-violence in China, the British maintained in deed and omission a nervous question mark over communist sovereignty. This was something that communist diplomats took more seriously as the 1950s unfolded, and especially as it became clear that 'special envoy' status would not be granted to a local political representative of the communist government in Hong Kong.

The British colonial indifference on how the KMT used their colony to strike back created a vacuum for Cultural Revolution communist violence to spill into Hong Kong in the 1967 riots. But that is another story. Lois Michison's prediction of an imminent, Hong Kong-based world war was popular in the mid-1950s. But it was far-fetched. Although the United States armed Taiwan with missiles, it also sponsored de-escalation by convincing the Kuomintang to abandon naval blockading positions on the Dachen Islands (off Zhejiang province) in 1955.[3]

This chapter begins by plotting out the various positions on who started the riot then describes the unsuccessful compensation case of Leung Tong, a forgotten victim of the riot, from a range of perspectives. In the case of the 1956 riot, those who could be thought much more squarely in the frame for riotous liability under the criminal law than the wives and mothers of the accidental dead were generally protected by their Rightist political orientation. This chapter makes no claim other than offering a description of how scapegoating worked in a British colony of East Asia in the mid-twentieth century, yet observes that, when legal fault was driven by political necessity, the colonial anatomy was at its most unconvincing. For a colonising people as reputedly law-loving as the British, it was damning to anyone who noticed.

Who started the riot of 1956?

An article in *Collier's* from 1951 described Hong Kong as a place 'full of people hanging around'.[4] It was 'the new Casablanca' with 'more spies per square foot than anywhere else in the world'.[5] In this storied locale, communists and KMT agents spied on each other, as well as on the Americans and the British, and vice versa. Do not forget the independent anti-communists. They were Rightist non-KMT guerrillas milling around Hong Kong who, along with KMT militarist factions, lived in hope of American aid for mainland reprisal campaigns.

Despite such a diverse milieu, an almost millennialist atmosphere prevailed in Hong Kong in the early 1950s. Not only did independent guerillas, cash-strapped and desperate, wait on American training and supplies, but KMT agents liked to put around a menace that 'anyone not actively pro-Kuomintang as well as anti-communist faces a dim future when Chiang Kai-shek returns to the mainland'.[6] Such cautioners were men and women who did not ordinarily resist colonialism in Hong Kong but communism in Hong Kong and the Chinese mainland. These people also resisted their impending political irrelevance. Many were former KMT soldiers adjusting to a less than glamourous life of poverty in a British enclave making them anxious about how quickly it was filling up with new, needy people. Flett reminded that 'the riot stands as an act of resistance to authority, or at least an aspect of it'.[7]

By 1956, life was, at last, looking better in the communist republic of China. It had overcome years in which it struggled to control the influence of KMT warlordism in southern China (1950–1952), saw mixed results from its second Five Year Plan (1953–1957), and was yet to plunge into the Great Leap Forward, a false start on industrialisation producing national famine (1958–1962). Not all was well in Hong Kong. The riot of 1956 occurred before the colony had returned fully to its reconstructed glory. Nor had it entirely shed its post-war image as an indolent bolt hole for arrivistes with a history of violence and holding disenchantment in their heart. In Hong Kong, the drifters had a small stake in the future because they wisely stayed in the colony and kept an allegiance to a dramatically smaller world. Hovering on the fringes of China, they grew bored of having nothing to do but inform on each other for a pittance. The British colony of Hong Kong was cosseted and cloistered, full of desperadoes hoping for deliverance, and ready to implode in a sharp click of air.

Throughout the late 1950s and early 1960s, the KMT had been reduced in its Hong Kong activities to a symbolic resistance of communism under the cloak of colonialism. In one incident, a small 'electrically operated' explosive device was detonated among the stalls of the Astor Theatre, Kowloon.[8] The eighty-five members of the mainland Mandarin Opera Company were performing there in a sold-out concert. Although the theatre was empty when the bomb went off, a left-wing newspaper reported Peking diplomatic representations to the British officials asking for the safety of the troupe to be secured by colonial authorities and 'severe punishment' to be handed out to 'Chiang's bandits'.[9]

The duration of a riot and its aftermath were fraught times for any colonial government. The anatomy of a riot played its role in restoring government authority without entirely laying to rest tensions between rival political groups or the suspicions they felt about each other. As Purdey pointed out, victims of a riot are seldom identified by the government as an 'exclusive' ethnic or political group but merely one included among a range of groups.[10] Hong Kong's 1956 riot was no different. It could not be portrayed by the colonial government as only the result of the KMT animating its gangster acolytes in a spree of violence and vandalism in a lightly veiled protest against the refugee influx. The outcome of the violence became generalised into nationalist tensions, and its causes and consequences shared by the colonial government between the KMT and the communists.

The official post-riot report found a suitable indeterminacy in the effects of the riot violence: '(in) assaults on persons and property both Europeans and Asians were victims of attack and both non-political and left wing buildings'.[11] Thus, the anatomy constructed by the colonial government of Hong Kong had to straddle indiscriminate loss and damage to property with its claim that the riot resulted from a turf war between two rival political factions. Anger arose in Peking as the result of the Governor's comment that it 'was unjust to ascribe the incidents to Nationalist agents'.[12] When asked to explain his comment, Peking made it clear that it was 'dissatisfied with the evasive replies of the British government'.[13]

Christine Loh's work gives a traditional description of the origins of the riot of 1956 in a dispute at Kowloon Refugee Reception Centre that escalated out of control.[14] A dispute about the erection of undescribed 'flags' in contravention of building regulations gave rise to a rain of rocks and the trashing of the centre's office, as well as subsequent spot fires of discontent becoming infernos throughout Sham Shui Po, Castle Hill and Tsuen Wan.[15] Another account blamed a resettlement department official for pulling down a political poster as the immediate cause of the riots.[16]

Given the colonial government's position that the communists and the nationalists shared in the blame for the riots, Loh seems careless that her finding that 'pro-nationalist supporters turned into an out of control mob'[17] rejects the Miners historiography which would lead one to believe that equal blame for the riot led to equal rebukes for the communists and KMT. Yet no such proposition could be further from the facts.

In Loh's account, the toll of the riot included around 6,000 arrests, 59 deaths and 443 people with injuries.[18] Governor Grantham's report noted two further deaths by gunshot wounds since his earlier report of 58 deaths making a total of 60 deaths and 89 wounded in hospital ten days after the riot.[19] Although Hung refers to the riot of 1956 as a 'rightist riot', he does not cover the communist outrage after the riot and sticks to the prescribed colonial historiography that it was 'suppressed by the British colonial government which had to maintain a delicate political balance between the two hostile political forces'.[20]

Tsang – after perusing a Colonial Office file – readily accepted that, 'as the government's inquiry into the 1956 disturbances concluded, the riots were not organized by the Kuomintang'.[21] He might be half-right. Understandably, arguing that Kuomintang was to blame for the riot, but could not be found fully liable for it by the British authorities, sounds a little too much like communist history. The problem with communist history is that even when it is probably right, it cannot entirely shake a suspicion that it indulges in a distortion.

A key aspect of the communist manipulation of history has been to coordinate and endlessly reiterate their disagreement with a colonial government, so they could burnish their representative or defensive posture in the history they wrote. Holding close to anti-feudalism and anti-imperialism as their watchwords, their policy on any point to a large extent made itself, however, there was seldom any public factionalism among the members of the communist tradition in dealings with a colonial government. This perfect fervency has a legacy in the incontrovertible way Chinese communists read history to this day: it is imbued by the familiarity of déjà vu.

More remarkable than an attribution of blame to the nationalists for the riot remaining ignored by the literature, Loh's work contains another controversial claim remaining untouched by everyone including the KMT Three of Dikötter, Tsang and Bickers and their camp-followers in doctoral purgatory. At one point, Loh gives credence to the communist position that during the riot 'the British had colluded with the KMT under American direction'.[22] Such a heresy has not been challenged because Western historiographical censoriousness these days occurs more by excluding Leftist recalcitrants from stage-managed discussions than by obviously warming one's hands to the KMT, although the likes of Dikötter and Tsang have quite flushed faces on that account.

The Euro-apologists writing, and encouraging writing, on Hong Kong have a taste for the pleasures of esoteric China. Paling beside the ambition of recent communist histories of Hong Kong, their shtick exhibits a culturally detached quality that made colonialism possible in the first place. Limited to topics such as treaty ports and customs duties, South China Sea piracy and anecdotes about abuses of extraterritoriality in the Chinese possessions, this literature treats the Far East as one big game of Monopoly. It devalues the centrality of law even in its most obviously political terrains. It necessarily avoids interpretations of ideology because it is compelled to defend sovereignty as if were not one, as if it were not a wicked or contrived invention but part of a natural order.

The average historian of treaty port China, and there are many of them, take an affected classicist's disdain for law's role in ideology. This is how they put it below the higher concerns of history. This means that the rules, say, of a post-riot compensation program cannot be a topic of interest. Nor is what the rules reveal about British biases, much less ideological motive. Philip Snow used to make the odd quip about self-interest among the parties to colonialism; Robert Bickers, too, on a rare day. Usually reading as a dim aside in a valley, not a journey to a sunlit upland, most historical writing on China dismisses theorists co-opting history as outlandish people with sinister or mistaken motives. And they quite often are, one way or another. But not always. It seems that an average historian's timidity congeals in equal suspicion of law as politics and the law of history.

Whether or not the local communists fought their KMT enemies hand-to-hand in the street, entered their headquarters with guns ablaze, they could not allow their part in the riot to be summed up by their enemies as an undisciplined corrective to colonial statism, or an indignant muscle flex inspired by Mao's outrage to Soviet leader Leonid Brezhnev's renunciation of Stalinism. Rather, they claimed that, although amply provoked by the Rightists, they did not join in a fight with them.[23]

Local representatives of the CCP had their own anatomy to formulate about the riot. In their view, cooperating with Hong Kong's police to get a better picture of who did what to whom in the riot could play no useful part in it. They were not really in pursuit of compensation but sought the moral mantle of speaking for Chinese people in the colony, and to give voice to their losses and continuing fears. Their main tactic was not to say things that any local Chinese would readily disagree with. They blended this nicely with an airy tone that came naturally to post-1949 communists, despite Mao's guidance to listen humbly to the ideas of non-members.

In his capacity of overseeing the consular affairs in Greater China, the British ambassador in Peking wrote a telegram to the Foreign Office referring to KMT agents 'who had immediately begun to collect gangsters and organize riots including attacks on shops, offices and schools' and that 'none of this was communist property'.[24] Citing a local informant, his telegram continued:

> The only communist agencies involved were the Hsinhua news agency which was besieged but not actually raided because employees held their ground and the bank of Kwangtung Province part of which was burnt down. The communists had been in a position of self-defence throughout the incidents. They had not surged out into the streets to fight back against the KMT special agents.[25]

This account was bound for the discretions of Whitehall, not the politics of Hong Kong. O'Neil did, however, refer to 'a serious disturbance' in the Tsuen Wan fabric and textile area 'where there was extensive fighting between opposing Chinese factions'.[26] On this slender reed, the Hong Kong government found the support it needed for its bi-partisan explanation of the riot's cause. The colonial government chose to muddy the causation issue to undermine compensatory demands of communists and position itself as a referee by preferring communist parity with the KMT in responsibility for the riots.

A CIA estimate noted that the communists were in up to their necks in intrigue and provocation during the riot years: 'during the summer and early fall of 1956 and at about the same time in 1959, communist pressures on Hong Kong increased markedly for a short time'.[27] The sporadic nature of communist post-war activism in Hong Kong was often correlated to their sensitivities about ongoing British relations with Taiwan. It would be naïve to suggest that communists were always blame-free when it came to disturbance-making. But the official colonial position that has been accepted by the historiography that the KMT and the communists fought a turf war over Hong Kong in 1956 has never been properly established, and certainly not by plumbing the depths and shallows of the archival references.

The British ambassador was not entirely alone in his general thrust of KMT blame for the riot. Lois Michison saw it thus:

> Most British newspapers have blamed last week's riots in Hong Kong on the impulsive hatred for communist organisations on the part of the Hong Kong's refugees from China. The Hong Kong government itself has talked of the Chinese secret societies using the riots to pay off old scores. Peking radio has blamed everything on 'KMT agents' using 'gangster elements' as a front. Peking radio blames everything from crop failure to sudden appendicitis on Kuomintang agents but this time it might be right.[28]

Although it is beyond the scope of this book, British colonial efforts to acculturate the refugee population of Hong Kong in the late 1950s should be seen as an exciting potential field for a study. How colonial authorities dealt with rootlessness and desperation among newly settled refugees could only shed new light on their colonial anatomy.

As nationalists of both stripes shared the blame for the riot, the communists bore their own losses caused by property damage. Many compensation claims for office damage of the communist trade unions in Castle Hill were denied on the basis of their refusal to make a full disclosure of sums already received in mitigation of their losses under 'Item 9 of Form A' of the compensation regime.[29] In British Hong Kong's loyalist newspapers, the communists were tilted between being virtually untouched by riot damage or presumptive co-authors of its most violent depredations depending on the stance needed by the colonial government anatomy at a particular moment. Given their tenuous hold on Hong Kong, it came somewhat as a revelation to British officials, however, that the attribution of the riot to something as touchy as Chinese nationalism had a place in their official anatomy. Despite common beliefs about divide and rule, in this case, it was a desperate move.

Part of the official role in preparing the anatomy of a riot was to traduce any person who would publish its obvious contradictions. 'Item 9, Form A' – the bureaucratic reason to deny compensation to communists – was, of course, little short of a colonial red herring. By colonial self-admission, the loss and damage claims were denied because the communists 'would not give further information to the police'.[30] The Deputy Colonial Secretary did not, however, want this line given further air: 'unless garbled versions of our replies appear in the left wing press or the matter is pursued publically in any way by the left wing, I would not personally favour any publicity'.[31]

In Hong Kong in 1956, the communist trade unions of Tsuen Wan suffered significant damage. In one case, the Spinning Workers' Union cited a damage bill amounting to HK$40,000 resulting from destruction of its 'workers' services centre'.[32] They made compensation claims, but were not paid. This was ostensibly because they refused to make statements about what payments had already received from insurers or overseas state sources.[33] Let it be entertained that this was the real reason for their denial of compensation. Laying down a flowchart of their connections to communist China for the delectation of colonial authorities would not be in the interests of local communists. The communist refusal to cooperate with police investigations would also fall into the category 'damned if you do, damned if you don't.' The high level of suspicion of colonial authorities of the Communist Party primed them to find evidence of bad faith in every corner of the communist camp.

Pointing the finger

No holiday, not even the Double Ten, creates conditions for a city-wide riot all by itself. Whitehall shared the Governor's view that it was unfair to ascribe the riot only to KMT nationalist agents.[34] Accordingly, 'HMG thought it rash for anybody including the Chinese government to make sweeping allegations about responsibilities'.[35] This infuriated senior members of the Chinese communist government who charged the British colonial administration with 'shielding and conniving with Nationalist agents'.[36]

Let it be said that, in the immediate aftermath of the riot, the British colonial administration wanted greatly to present the riot as a turf war between the KMT and the communist-controlled trade unions in Hong Kong. This could deflect from its embarrassing laxity in controlling the KMT's use of the colony as a base for U.S.-backed sabotage operations in southeast China and be chalked up as the Chinese communists showing Brezhnev how they could lead the communist world. This formed an irresistible context for communist involvement in the riots, although false and opportunist.

The Chinese communists played smart politics by pushing hard on the riot compensation issue. There was ample truth to the claim that colonial government did not take care of Chinese people within its jurisdiction. When the *South China Morning Post* made its splash about the government's compensation scheme, its inadequacy was obvious despite the generous write-up. Despite shelling out 'nearly one and half million dollars' and taking into account 'compassionate grounds', Justice T.J. Gould presided over a Riot Compensation Advisory Board that paid on average HK$4,000 to relatives of the deceased when the workers' compensation comparator for death was HK$10,000. Dependants of persons killed (22 cases) received a total of $91,900 and the 16 cases in the KMT factory sector amounted to HK$1,159,562 (unhelpfully called by the *Post* story 'Major Claims in respect of damage premises and loss of stocks and vehicles').[37] The cases decided on compassionate grounds constituted by half-payments to individuals (ten or so cases), who did not satisfy all evidentiary requirements, amounted to $23,720.[38] The value of property has always exceeded that attributed to human life in the Chinese tradition, and the British administration could claim it was merely following suit.

When the communist Chinese regarded Hong Kong in the 1950s, they saw four out of five people living in poverty and one in five enjoying practically unlimited access to the technical possibilities of intellectualism. The riot of 1956 was not politically Rightist in aim or execution, but was started and propelled by Rightists frustrated by the social conditions of the colony seen as being caused by the excess of refugees. The communist response to the riot focussed on the treatment of victims as members of a community in name only whose colonial government saw as too numerous to be part of its modernity project. But they were also too numerous to ignore when calculating initiatives to increase the political stability of the colony. This numerical contradiction challenged the colonial anatomy of ordered progress and benign distribution in the period 1956–1957.

The CCP had eyes and ears everywhere in Hong Kong, and was quite prepared to use its intelligence to mount a political argument with colonial Hong Kong in 1956. The communist Chinese Vice Minister alleged:

> two nationalist agents were in the Political Department of the Hong Kong Police and that the Hong Kong authorities were also in contact with the Kuomintang 'Commissioner' Wu Wen-hut.[39]

To this, the Vice Minister added unrefuted allegations of British involvement intrigues such as the Kashmir Princess, nationalist jet aircraft and the case of 'KMT agents trained in Hong Kong who had attempted sabotage in Canton'.[40] When read literally, the reply to this of Alan Lennox-Boyd, Secretary of State for the Commonwealth, could only be described as evasive about the events of the past:

> I was very willing to repeat the assurance that I had already given to the Prime Minister that Hong Kong authorities had no intention of allowing Hong Kong agents or anybody else to use the territory of Hong Kong to interfere with or menace China.[41]

In his next telegram to the Governor, Lennox-Boyd blames the mutual policy of an open border for KMT acts in mainland China:

> The Hong Kong government cannot be responsible for the credentials of all those leaving Hong Kong for China as they are free to do in accordance with what we understand to be the wishes of the Chinese government as well as HMG. [42]

The most alarming observation a Chinese communist could make to a colonial power was that it had lost control of its colony. The flurry of British denials responded to such an implication. The British appeal to the impracticality of border control into China suggests that KMT agents arriving to wreak havoc in nearby Canton were not there courtesy of a moonless airborne drop from a C-47 Skytrain risking communist airspace. Nor were they teleported through time and space. They might on occasion have come in from Burma or Macau, but the most convenient border crossing was Hong Kong's.

One British journalist reported that military authorities were in disagreement with the civil authorities as to the timing of when to call out the troops. He was publically rebuked for this reporting because it was 'unwittingly providing material for communist China'.[43] The Chinese vice-minister for foreign affairs, speaking on the authority of Zhou Enlai, noted the near loss through 'encirclement and threat' of the Kwangtung Bank and the New China News Agency (Xinhua) 'until the police eventually arrived'.[44] This characterisation was taken by colonial authorities to be 'the Chinese government making political capital out of the situation'.[45] The vice-minister (Zhang Hangfu) claimed that in his nation's reportage he had 'attempted to minimise the gravity of the riots and the threats', but that the gravity of the situation was due to the British shielding the elements responsible for the riots, namely the KMT.[46]

A hapless civilian and his widow

The introduction suggested that something can be learned about the anatomy of the riot, and its role in the formulation of colonial ideology, by studying compensation claims made in Hong Kong in 1957. On 12 October 1956, an incident took place at the height of the Hong Kong riots that put the anatomy at odds with a popular account. A dead man's wife said he was an innocent trying to get home; the government implied he was a looter who got more than he bargained for. Such a disagreement could hardly be surprising in a riot. A government pulled from a riot only those lessons it needed to fortify its law and order prescriptions, or deflect blame from a proxy. There was no such thing as indeterminate violence or a mistake made in the use of force. Presumably, in the case of Mr Leung Tong, there could be no acceptable explanation of his being in the wrong place at the wrong time when such a mistake was made.

Colonial governments often dealt with widows. The bereaved often sought some sort of accountability for loss of their breadwinner. An antithetical 'side' was easily assumed by colonial forces and given the power to pronounce an unmourned death over any who would ignore its prescription of law and order. A colonial government was compelled to present a riot as a steady anatomy, a calm retelling of disordered events, and an attribution of blame safe on the footings of reason and justice. This is why the anatomy of a riot was the hardest ideological project for a colonial government to undertake. It had to appear authoritative but it had special problems including new circumstances constantly being revealed in the media, and legitimately quarrelsome individuals undermining any projection of the government's restraint and objectivity. Yet the treatment of those caught in the fog of the riot, such as Mr Leung and his widow, leave an impression, not of a victim, but a scapegoat.

The victim

Mr Leung's wife, Mrs Ho Mo Ching, was not satisfied by the response of the colonial government to her compensation claim. Deciding to retain a lawyer and write to the compensation board, she asked whether her husband was considered to have committed crimes during the riot or if she had not submitted enough evidence to support her claim of loss of livelihood:

> I am 50 years old and living with the deceased's son Leung Kuin Hung who is only 12 years old solely depends on the deceased who was a good civilian. I trust you confirm this by checking records in police stations. Examination of his body would have shown what I say is true. Since his death we have found ourselves in extreme destitution and can hardly maintain our living. I beg most respectfully for your kindest reconsideration.[47]

Mrs Ho was not officially among the people of Hong Kong officially sharing in $1,478,956 of the victims' property, death or maiming compensation awarded in the wake of the Hong Kong riots of 1956.[48] A file note in her compensation claim noted that her lawyer was the ordinarily non-partisan Mr Peter Mo and that '[her] letter does not quite amount to what was argued in the left wing Press'.[49] There were seventy other maiming or death compensation claims that were rejected by the compensation board.[50] For a colonial administration braced by a set of rules permitting no ambiguity in who would be compensated for loss of life during the riot, this comment that the widow's claim was not being used by her cynically in the press strikes an odd note.

Mrs Ho's claim that her husband was untarnished by a criminal record was not thought conclusive. For what they were worth, British colonial statistics claimed that 5,226 people were arrested in connection with the riots for curfew breaking, rioting or unlawful assembly, only 1,240 had previous criminal records – about one quarter.[51] In this sense, the statistical argument was not on the side of Mrs Ho. But in another sense, Mrs Ho and her husband were unlucky. There were 1,455 arrests for breaching curfew orders, and 1,241 people were sent to prison for up to two months.[52] Given the scale of the property damage and civil disobedience, deaths during the riot were quite rare.

The police

The Police agreed with Leung Tong's widow that he approached Cheung Sha Wan Road and Yuen Chau St on 12 October 1956 at around 2:30 p.m. But from that point onward, their stories diverged. In the height of a riot this might be expected, if not quite such a marked difference in the accounts. Leung was alleged by the police to have run at full stretch toward them, and the soldiers at the junction, establishing a narrative that his fate was self-induced. Police challenged him to stop. He continued to run past the roadblock. He was challenged again. Again, he failed to stop. He was shot near the crossroad by one of the soldiers with a rifle. Both accounts also agree that he died in Sham Shui Po Police Station of his injuries that night in the company of other suspected rioters. Neither the police nor military forces assembled at the checkpoint released any further details, including any results of an autopsy if performed on the deceased.

Joint anti-riot deployments of the military and the police throughout Kowloon Peninsula on 11–12 October 1956 received little or no critique in either the popular broadsheets or the official histories of the riot. Rather, a tone of calm exoneration covers the record like a fine dust:

> the officers of the Colony's regular garrison conducted themselves in a commendably forbearing and good humoured manner but with a degree of firmness and resolution which was one of the main factors in the very rapid collapse of the large scale disorder.[53]

If anyone was to harbour the slightest doubt after this, the report notes: 'the military forces did not find it easy to open fire at any stage while they were on duty in Kowloon and Tsuen Wan'.[54]

At the time and place of Leung Tong's death, there was no suggestion of politics by its colonial defenders or in reports of internecine conflicts that engulfed neighbourhoods, just unexplained riotous mayhem. Not even a Swiss consul being dragged from his car and murdered in broad daylight could be described in an anti-colonial light.[55] Innocent or not, Mr Leung Tong walked or ran into trouble. The military account described generally what he encountered on the afternoon of 12 October:

> during the period up to 2.00pm the whole of the area south and south west of Li Cheng Uk as far as the sea and south east beyond the junction was the scene of general and serious rioting with many cases of arson, looting and attacks on persons and property. The Sham Shui Po Post Office was attacked and many cars were set on fire.[56]

Mr Leung opted to take an innocent walk through an apocalypse, or was ambushed by it, or was a rioter: these remain the options.

History and anatomy

Unlike a police officer or a compensation claimant, a historian is compelled to hold a view inferred from a body of evidence. Who started the riot of 10–12 October 1956, to where it spread, and how the government responded to restore law and order, were all perfectly understandable matters in their own right. Yet no such segment necessarily shed light on why the riot occurred at all or the political motive for legalised blame. In deciding to sub-title this book *Anatomy of a Riot*, the concern here for colonial government's interpretation of a riot's aftermath, and its politics generally, is *as if* something from which underlying realities can be inferred. In such a narrative, why riot compensation was payable to one, but not another, is a sensible reference guide.

No colonial government's response to a riot could amount to a mute lack of attribution or resolute denial of any compensation at all. Late colonialism as a form of government could not be satisfied with the recollection that a riot ended because it briefly unleashed its colossus of terror until every other type of violence struggled for air. Only by offering a tolerably accurate account of murderer and innocent, or participant and victim, can a riot become part of the government's story of order and justice. That is in large part missing from the riot of 1956, because too much faith was put by the colonial administration in blaming both communist and KMT adherents alike. From the point of view of a historian, the colonially decided specifics of nationalist violent intent sit uneasily with the messy reality of a riot. Birchall reminded us that a riot usually involves 'hundreds, perhaps thousands of individuals whose motivations and interactions are too complex to grasp'.[57]

If one is to call the violence of 1956 KMT-led or Rightist gangster-inspired, the riot must also about violence as a refusal to accept you have lost a larger political fight. Nihilistic resistance might be the only way to describe the motives of those who sparked the 1956 riot. Some violence was aimed by its perpetrators to create an epistemological shift, or make a fresh show of consequence for a government ignoring a grievance about overcrowding. In the end, however, their violence merely advertised their futility. In this sense, the perpetrators of violence were the last to know they were nihilists. The same cannot be said of the British colonial government.

For the KMT in Hong Kong and southern China, the 1956 riot was among the earlier throws of the dice that would result in a determinative crackdown by the British in 1963. As an incident of history, the riot was an example of the British reinforcing their colonialism in Hong Kong in part by hosting KMT Rightists uncritically from 1945 to 1963. At the same time, the United Kingdom was among the first of nations recognising P.R. China in 1950. Such contradiction could not fail to give British colonialism in Hong Kong an ambiguous aura – even to the eye of an average treaty port historian amusing themselves over jade novelties and sepia prints of tennis parties.

Under its anatomy, the colonial corpus encountered new stimuli and needed to recognise its own slow rate of learning. But this implied amendment of key claims that had seemed immutable to its diehards. By early 1960s, there could no longer be KMT bystanders, nor partisan subjects to receive colonial compensation or exoneration from criminal penalty. The anatomy, as always, gave high recognition to a species of Chinese need best represented by self-absorbed landlords fleeing imminent threat to their health and well-being, who had to seek domicile in Hong Kong as exiled mobsters on diminished means. But politically adherent KMT types among them could not ignore a gradually increasing shortness of British patience for their activities after the riot of 1956.

The Chinese communists and their Hong Kong proxies played a masterful hand after 1956. Their complaints of inadequate compensation acted as a smoke screen. In one senior colonial discussion about whether Hong Kong should follow Malaya's example by banning communist organisations and hunting them down, it was decided that they did not pose sufficient threat.[58] This position became formalised in Grantham's equal diffidence policy of 1948 and did not change officially until after the Cultural Revolution-inspired riots of 1967.

The questions raised by the Leung Tong assault are many and embarrassing. They will never be answered properly, yet when compiled and combined can produce a powerful inference about why an anatomy of a riot could accept no bystanders. For a historian, when evidential indeterminacy becomes presumed guilt, colonialism does not so much hit a new low, as it unconsciously reveals its illegitimacy. It is important to catalogue the questions that expose realities beneath the anatomy.

Anatomical questions

The cause of a riot was often attributed by a British colonial administration to hotheads or rascals becoming over-exuberant. Much to the irritation of China's communist leaders, Hong Kong's riot in 1956 was variously characterised by the colonial government as a 'factional fight'[59] and 'strife'[60] between the KMT and communist-led trade unions. John Young accepted this into his history without a single doubt: 'the people involved were part of the struggle . . . between the Chinese Communists and the nationalists'.[61] By promoting such an account, the colonial administration staked its claim to be a sensible voice of business and progress forced by an irreparable political cleavage to step in and stop internecine killing. As such, the anatomy of British colonialism in 1950s Hong Kong was not contentious: it was a perfectly acceptable construct to those sending out invitations to the historiography club.

In this section, a series of naïve questions developed from the documentary silences in the Leung case is posed to develop a contrarian interpretive approach to the riot of 1956 – one that is other than that supplied by mainland and local communists, or the colonial government, but highlighting the colonial anatomy nevertheless. In the case of Hong Kong's riot in 1956, the colonial administration emphasised the political aspect so that its patchy criminal sanctions against rioters would receive less scrutiny than otherwise they could have done.

Communist misgivings along skeptical lines were conceivably too numerous and specific to be entirely discounted: 'Yeung Tat Yang one of the notorious culprits in riots last year . . . openly made his appearance again in Tsuen Wan again last month'.[62] However, there is a plausible way to see the events of 1956 and 1957 that reveals an aspect of the colonial anatomy willing to attribute liability to powerless people and do so with no reference to due process. This could indicate that the politically unaligned were criminalised or left cold to protect the politically favoured as an underlying mode of British colonialism in the colony.

Few of the questions that may be asked about Leung's death will be surprising. Yet they have a quality of a touchstone. Highlighting differences between Hong Kong's anatomical façade and a reasonable, if subjective, idea of justice, Leung's case reveals colonial indifference that can be probed for elsewhere in the corpus. There are quite obvious questions that can be asked by a disappointed claimant that peel away the anatomy and reveal quite a disconcerting state of affairs.

Why is there no mention from the government side about whether or not Leung actually had a police record? Was this not followed up, or was verification of the widow's claim thought a risk to the government's point of view? The government statistics recognising high levels of free abandon in the riot are not reliable to determine guilt of riotous behaviour in an individual case.

If Mr Leung was ill and unarmed, why was he running at a fully armed government barricade? The contemporaneous government account of the riot refers to rioters avoiding checkpoints and 'outflanking' or 'doubling back' to commercial areas in side streets to pillage.[63] Running at an armed checkpoint on the final day of a riot seems insane, and not true to the established practice of rioters in the 1956 riot.

Why did Leung's cause of death remain unspecified? It was quite common for accidental Chinese deaths to have no autopsy report, even in the 1960s, but a death in a riot holds a different claim to truth than, say, a so-called coolie accidentally reversed over by a truck in a loading bay. The widow's letter claimed that he 'eventually died' at the police station and she was informed he was 'brought for anatomical treatment' to a morgue.[64]

Had an autopsy been performed on Leung, and there was no evidence that it was, it should matter to the colonial government whether he had died from a bullet or a gas shell. Why was the government's silence in the manner of his death not quizzed more fully by the compensation claimant? Or was it a case of proceeding softly, softly in hope of partial compensation? Tear gas was usually deployed as a defensive resort designed to demoralise and disperse massed people. Could it have been deployed by accident, or was Leung in the thick of riotous behaviour, or simply trying to make his way home amidst the crazy pageant of the riot?

On the colonial account, as well as the widow's, Leung was alive when taken to the police station. Was he not given medical treatment when he arrived there because he was considered a rioter? It seems quite likely. Instead of helping him, Mr Leung – doubtlessly writhing uncomfortably in his last moments – was dragged off, deposited in the back of a truck and dumped in a cell to die. There was a military hospital in Kowloon fully prepared for casualties. Not taking him there was the beginning of the adverse judgment made against him.

The standard evidenced claim was for $4,000 for personal injury causing death to be given to a dependent.[65] The government's file note had observed that Mrs Ho was not in league with the Leftist newspapers by fanning its suspicions of the causes of her husband's death. Did this mean she was paid, say, a fraction of the full award on compassionate grounds, as was the case in some insufficiently evidenced claims? There seems a reasonable prospect of this. In fact, there was documentary evidence that the colonial administration paid ex-gratia compensation payments after the main compensation sums were awarded and that the practice continued until March 1958.[66] This was based on a legal option open to the compensation board to 'relieve all cases of genuine hardship suffered by genuine persons' which amounted to 50 percent of an ordinary award and given on 'compassionate grounds'.[67]

The Freilich thesis

A large anatomical question in these pages concerns the legitimacy of a colonial government in a riot. Of course, who started a riot, and what their motives or demands were, has entered the academic discourse before. The significance of the riot in Hong Kong, however, lays in the colonial government's political reaction to it. In this matter, I challenge a norm about riots that many readers will take for granted in a Western, democratic context. Much of our understanding of civil disobedience, riotous behaviour and all acts in between has been conditioned by the constitutionally prescribed certainties of the Western democratic condition. Much of this thinking transposes much too easily to considering a riot in a colonial context, as if a colonial government's democratic authority or representation of community decency was at stake.

When called on to define legitimate civil disobedience in the context of America in the late 1960s, Robert Freilich ventured that it was open and public, rose above limited self-interest through 'moral justification and conscience', was not guided by a primary intent to lawlessness, was conducted by people willing to accept legal punishment to invoke a community sense of injustice and avoided 'all forms of violence and interference with rights of third persons'.[68]

Freilich saw civil disobedience as 'a viable alternative to violence and revolution'[69] when 'lawful forms of dissent may not be adequate to disturb or raise the conscience of the public to reform the laws'.[70] However, the government type that concerned Freilich was late American constitutionalism, which, he nevertheless warned, 'commands obedience only so long as its blessings are not too high a price for law and order'.[71] Evidence of such relativism might be laudable in a constitutional Western state, but circumstances were much different from those obtaining in a colony.

What should happen, then, when a group of foreigners came to your land and imposed their authoritarian dictates on you and enforced racist social control of your life chances? What can be said of the rights of parties to their life and property in a riot in such a context? Surely, if a right to resist colonialism is recognised, then the political proximity of an individual to such a despotism has influence on who might be properly thought an innocent bystander in a riot. It also means that the dependants of a bona fide innocent treated badly by a colonial government after a riot assumes high importance.

There's a larger question derived from Freilich: can there be a right of rioters to engage in violence and revolution when their government maintained despotic and discriminatory attitudes sustained by the theft of their birthright? The reality underlying a colonial anatomy in an outpost such as Hong Kong puts insurrection against its orderings of property in quite a different place to those presumed normal in a democratic constitutional state.

In October 1956, Hong Kong was no kind of democracy. The riot was no kind of conventional political protest, either. In its aftermath, it was an example of colonial despotism trying to accommodate Rightist nihilism. Freilich contended, 'a democracy cannot be maintained by passive obedience to all law nor by [people] unwilling to take to the streets when ordinary debate is discouraged or ineffectual.'[72] An authoritarian colonial government can and often did demand passive obedience to all law, for it was based on the rule of the police officer and the garrison. Yet because of this, and because ordinary debate was routinely put down and became useless, resort by colonised people to violence and terrorism must be seen as an exception to the neo-liberal, post-colonial edict belabouring the importance of internationalism and pacifism in the search for self-determination as ever it does. Violence and revolution have been and remain the only ways forward for a self-realising people not given to compromise. Such reasoning could put the Cultural Revolution-inspired 1967 riot in Hong Kong in a new light. It leaves the one in 1956 as something of a partisan embarrassment to the British because its damaging aftermath could have been avoided by actually following the colonial anatomy of equal indifference.

Conclusion

The mystery of Mr Leung's death hangs over this chapter. I suspect it will never be solved. Yet many aspects of the Hong Kong Riot of 1956 stand in a clearer light because of his case. It demonstrated how an anatomy of a riot was constructed and how it would be exceedingly fragile if it could not rely on a lack of accountability of police to answer the most basic questions. It illustrated in a single case the capacity of a colonial government to assume a set story with little or no concern for its truth, and showed how the unrecognised innocence of the indeterminate masked the guilt of the guilty.

No colonial government could leave conclusions of indeterminate riot violence to prevail. There must be a constituency threatened by an intentioned evil. The government's job must be to protect its public against such an evil with reassuring moments of martial finality or pennies from heaven for old friends. The case of Leung Tong demonstrated that a riot could produce more than one account with a passing claim to be factual, and that determined blame of innocents was not an unthinkable way to keep the price of the compensation bill down, and chums out of jail.

After giving a report of the riots from an auxiliary military perspective, first-hand witness Godfrey Dykes concluded on 16 October 1956 'all is well now and the rich whites are back to normal riotous living in Hong Kong'.[73] Of course, the elite beneficiary role of the Europeans in the extraction of wealth from Hong Kong could never find its way explicitly into the colonial anatomy. It could only be about properly constituted systems delivering measurable benefits to colonial subjects on principles of merit and compassion. This was the fraught anatomy of compensation after the riot of 1956.

Colonial government authority based itself on assumed European racial superiority. After the Second World War, Winston Churchill was adamant that the sovereignty referred to in the Atlantic Charter was that of Britain over its colonies, not that possessed by its colonial subjects to form independent nations.[74] Resulting from this was a range of policy positions on trade and economic development in colonies relegated these days by the historiography of Empire to odd spasms arresting the timely fruition of human rights and individual dignity, as if the likes of Cobden and Bright had been justifiably ignored in their day. Prejudicial policies of the colonies were nevertheless effective in their time as measured signals about who had a place at the table of government, and why. Leung's case suggested as much.

A colonial state's tally keepers were frontline in a riot's anatomy. Witness the activities of the military and the police who made their contemporaneous reports, or the insurers who received the earliest access to the damage and its estimates. Also observe the commissioners of inquiry who were given every assistance in establishing terms of reference, and a pile of cash, along with lawyers and other intellectuals tamed by the commercial opportunities of a colony. All these people possessed different ways of quantifying harm, but shared the same political code for expressing its consequence. In this scene, a sociologist or historian cuts a lonely figure. Kept outside the police incident tape, a seeker of causes can wait years for the papers supporting the official report to come out. When a reading of them gives no support to an explanation of state innocence, or a media-stoked myth that compensation was ample and principled, the facts of an individual's fight for justice can take its place as a modest claim for some truth. Leung's case suggested as much.

The Hong Kong colonial anatomy did not see itself through – or compare itself with – other ideological representations of colonialism. Despite its complete assurance, in its flow charts linking processes to expert panels and justice, such things were about how to put its best people in the front row as if this were the first and last time a colonial state would need to do so. Such processes, although conceiving themselves as ad hoc, have caused a grim humour about unfairness as if a malady of the British specifically, and raised unflattering questions about how the world viewed them as rulers in system rather than incident.

Colonial government was a finely calibrated 'yes' or 'no' machine based so heavily on armed force that many in it rightly wondered whether conceding 'yes' to any 'native' suggestion was quite necessary when it risked dividing the spoils with another race. It was the subjectiveness of the British modus that was common to every chapter of their empire's anatomy. This was what Lao Tzu called 'private ends' dressed up as something else. The examples in the preface made it clear that the private ends were massive KMT property compensation payments at the expense of compensating individual deaths and injury.

A riot was judged by the cold eye of expected civil restraint and its assured lines of reward. This was not to be mistaken for fairness. The aftermath of a riot was carried by the fine myth of disinterested anatomy. Why some people deserved compensation afterward, and others were outside the deserving corpus, were not matters for scrutiny if you wanted to be part of the colonial enterprise. Of course, in the official explanation, the anatomy of all that was good and functional, only a colonial state's allies were measurably set back by the riot. Everyone else was a perpetrator, or under its ogre of suspicion or languishing, futile and indeterminate. The anatomy of a riot enacted the purest colonial venality. The good-old-chap back slaps hid behind a veil of impartial legality proven by nothing more than its colonial assertion.

Who was implicated in riotous lawlessness should have been crucial to the questions of compensation and criminal retribution, but we will note in the next chapter that they were not. In the aftermath of the 1956 riot, the KMT prevailed, but the communists did not lose ultimately. We noted the strongest colonial administration reaction during the riot was to a British reporter's assertion that the troops were late in being called out. In the colonial government's characterisation of events, the riot was a political turf war between the KMT and the Chinese communists. Any suggestion that it had, for any period of time, lost control of its colony to gangs of criminal tuffs was un-British.

The case of Mr Leung presented a docket of incidents ignored by the compensation authority. It started with a presumption he was a rioter and would climb down from that position only if necessary. The anatomy, as in colonial life in general, relied less on discriminatory application of rules per se than on a collective colonial imagination that a presumption of innocence was wasted on non-white people. This made supportive Chinese business people the best bet in the colonial enterprise because their self-interest could be predicted. On the disparaging side of the colonial imaginary, non-whites were always 'up to something', or less capable than whites of self-discipline, or unable to sensitively pursue constitutional rights. That was the fight of Leung's widow.

The fluidity and contingency of British recognition of the communist government of China and the KMT was the seedy reality that lay beneath the British anatomy of equal indifference to both. In 1955, the Chinese government requested that the British recognise an Office of Special Envoy that the communists proposed to set up in Hong Kong.[75] Rejecting this, Governor Grantham had suggested the Chinese government set up a consulate, but Zhou Enlai could not agree to it because it implied that Hong Kong was a foreign territory to the Chinese government.[76] Wesley-Smith suggested that Grantham's reluctance was for the practical reason of it being hard to distinguish for consular assistance purposes between Hong Kong residents of Chinese descent and Chinese nationals.[77] This view does

not tally with at least one Foreign Office memo in 1963 in which British
officials admitted to relying on communist intelligence to find KMT operatives in Hong Kong.[78] To the Chinese communists, Hong Kong residents
did not all look the same, and if they did so to the British officials, they
should not be afraid to ask for communist help. In 1963, that's exactly
what the British did.

Notes

1 HKRS 163-1-2029 3/811/57; 389/1459855: 'Payment Arrangements
   for Riot Compensation'.
2 Keith Flett (ed), *A History of Riots* (Newcastle: Cambridge Scholars Publishing, 2015), 3.
3 Bill Brugger, *China: Liberation and Transformation 1942–1962* (London:
   Croom Helm, 1981), 105.
4 Robert Shaplen, 'Guerrillas – Our Hope in Red China' *Collier's* (21
   July 1951), 14.
5 Shaplen, 16.
6 Shaplen, 16.
7 Flett, 2.
8 HKMS 158-1-283: CO 1030/1605: 'Extract LIC Report for May'.
9 HKMS 158-1-283: CO 1030/1605: 'Extract LIC Report for May' and
   'Sir R Black to Secretary of State for Commonwealth' (8 July 1963).
10 Jemma Purdy, 'The "Other" May Riots: Anti-Chinese Violence in Solo,
   May 1998' in Charles Coppel (ed), *Violent Conflicts in Indonesia: Analysis,
   Representation, Resolution* (London: Routledge, 2006), 82.
11 HKMS 158-3-1: 'Foreign Office Far Eastern Dept 1954–6 Disturbances in
   Kowloon (Disturbances, Riots and Incidents) 440/01', [1].
12 HKMS 158-3-1: 'Telegram 3: Secretary of State for the Commonwealth
   Alan Lennox-Boyd to Sir A. Grantham' (20 October 1956), [3].
13 HKMS 158-3-1: 'Telegram 3', [3].
14 Christine Loh, *Underground Front: The Chinese Communist Party in Hong
   Kong* (Hong Kong: Hong Kong University Press, 2010), 87.
15 Loh, 87.
16 HKPF, *History of Hong Kong Police* website: 'The Modern Era' Avail.
   at: www.police.gov.hk/info/doc/history/chapter02_en.pdf (accessed: 1
   August 2018), 3.
17 Loh, 87.
18 Loh, 87.
19 HKMS 158-3-1: 'Foreign Office Far Eastern Dept 1954–6 Disturbances in
   Kowloon (Disturbances, Riots and Incidents) 440/01': 'Telegram (2) Sir
   A Grantham to SoSC' (22 October 1956).
20 Steven Chung-fun Hung, 'Interest Groups and Democracy Movement in
   Hong Kong: A Historical Perspective' in Sonny Shiu Hing Lo (ed), *Interest
   groups and the New Democracy Movement in Hong Kong* (Oxon: Routledge,
   2018), 26.
21 Steve Tsang, 'Strategy for Survival: The Cold War and Hong Kong's Policy Toward Kuomintang and Chinese Communist Activities in the 1950s'
   Journal of Imperial and Commonwealth History vol. 25, no. 2, 2008: 304.

22 Loh, 87.
23 HKMS 158-3-1: 'Telegram 3', [3].
24 HKMS 158-3-1: 'Telegram 1', [1].
25 HKMS 158-3-1: 'Telegram 1', [1].
26 HKMS 158-3-1: 'Telegram 1', [10].
27 CIA-RDP79-R00904A000500020099-9: 'Memorandum for the Director, Validity of Present Estimate on Hong Kong SNIE 13–3–57, The Chinese Communist Threat to Hong Kong, date 19 November 1957' (16 February 1960), [3].
28 Lois Michison, 'Hong Kong Riots' *New Statesman and Nation* (20 October 1956), 5.
29 HKRS 163-1-2029 CR/811/57: 'Payment Arrangements for Riot Compensation'; HKRS 163-1-2029; 526/57/58: 'Communist Accounts': Hongkong Kowloon Chinese Farming and Agriculture Association to Colonial Secretary'.
30 HKRS 163-1-2029 CR/811/57: 'Payment Arrangements for Riot Compensation'.
31 HKRS 163-1-2029: 'Deputy Colonial Secretary to Commissioner of Compensation' (18 September 1957).
32 HKRS 163-1-2029: 'Communist Accounts'.
33 HKRS 163-1-2029 526/57/58: 'Communist Accounts': 'Hongkong Kowloon Chinese Farming and Agriculture Association to Secretary for the Commonwealth'.
34 HKMS 158-3-1 440/01: 'Telegram 3: Secretary of State for Colonies Alan Lennox-Boyd to Sir A. Grantham' (20 October 1956), [2].
35 HKMS 158-3-1 440/01: 'Telegram 4: Secretary of State for the Commonwealth Alan Lennox-Boyd to Sir A. Grantham' (20 October 1956), [2].
36 HKMS 158-3-1 440/01: 'Telegram 3', [2].
37 HKRS 163-1-2029 (523/57/58): 'Riot Compensation Report' ('Cutting from SCMP' dated 28 August 1957).
38 HKRS 163-1-2029 (523/57/58): 'Cutting from SCMP'.
39 HKMS 158-3-1 440/01: 'Telegram 3'.
40 HKMS 158-3-1 440/01: 'Telegram 3'.
41 HKMS 158-3-1 440/01: 'Telegram 4'.
42 HKMS 158-3-1: 'Telegram 5: SoSC to Sir A. Grantham' (20 October 1956), [4].
43 HKMS 158-3-1 21/10/56: 'Sir A. Grantham to Secretary of State for the Commonwealth' (22 October 1956).
44 HKMS 158-3-1 440/01: 'Telegram 3', [4].
45 HKMS 158-3-1 440/01: 'Telegram 3', [4].
46 HKMS 158-3-1 440/01: 'Telegram 3', [4].
47 HKRS 163-1-2029; DFS(F) 23 April 1958: 'Payment Arrangements'.
48 HKRS 163-1-2029; DFS(F) 23 April 1958: 'Payment Arrangements'.
49 HKRS 163-1-2029; DFS(F) 23 April 1958: 'Payment Arrangements'.
50 HKRS 163-1-2029; DFS(F) 23 April 1958: 'Payment Arrangements'.
51 HKMS 158-3-1; 440/01: 'Telegram 2: Sir A Grantham to SoSC 22 October 1956'.
52 HKPF, Hong Kong police website.
53 PRO52562: 'Report Covering the Involvement of British and Gurkha Troops during the Civil Disturbances of 1956, 1966 and 1967' (British Forces Post Office Hong Kong, 1987), [53].

54 PRO52562: [53].
55 PRO52562: [34].
56 PRO52562: [33].
57 Ian Birchall, 'Imagined Violence: Some Riots in Fiction' in Keith Flett (ed), *A History of Riots* (Newcastle: Cambridge Scholars Publishing, 2015), 39.
58 HKRS 184-4-21; 1948 JKS, 24/6/1948: 'Kuomintang Activities': 'It remains to be seen how long we will be able to tolerate the steady growth of the Communist Party but I agree that until we have occasion in Hong Kong to deal firmly with the communist element on the lines that it now appears to be dealt with in Malaya, the Governor's policy of letting Hong Kong be a "free for all" so long as individuals don't cause trouble in Hong Kong is probably the best one'.
59 HKMS 158-3-1: 'Telegram 3: Secretary of State for the Commonwealth to Sir A. Grantham' (20 October 1956).
60 HKMS 158-3-1: 'Telegram 1: Mr O'Neil (Peking) to Foreign Office' (16 October 1956), [2].
61 John Young, 'The Building Years: Maintaining a China-Hong Kong-Britain Equilibrium, 1950–1971' in Ming Chan (ed), *Precarious Balance Hong Kong Between China and Britain 1842–1992* (Hong Kong: Hong Kong University Press, 1994), 139.
62 HKRS163-1-2029 (523/57/58): 'Communist Accounts' in 'Workers Protest Against Riot Compensation' (*Ta Kung Pao* articles, 31 August 1957).
63 PRO52562, [34].
64 HKRS 163-1-2029; 3/811/57.
65 HKRS 163-1-2029; DFS(F) 23 April 1958.
66 HKRS410-10-9: 'Riot Compensation Payments – Ex-Gratia Payments'.
67 HKRS 163-1-2029; DFS(F) 23April 1958.
68 Robert Freilich, 'The Emerging General Theory of Civil Disobedience Within the Legal Order' in Richard Chikorta and Michael Moran (eds), *Riot in the Cities: An Analytical Symposium on the Causes and Effects* (Rutherford: Fairleigh Dickinson University Press, 1970), 79.
69 Freilich, 79.
70 Freilich, 76.
71 Freilich, 81.
72 Freilich, 78.
73 Godfrey Dykes, Godfrey Dykes personal website, 'Hong Kong – October 1956'. Avail. at: www.godfreydykes.info/HONG%20KONG%20 1956.pdf (accessed: 14 January 2018).
74 Lawrence James, *The Rise and Fall of the British Empire* (London: Abacus, 1994), 502.
75 Loh, 81.
76 Loh, 81.
77 Peter Wesley-Smith, 'Chinese Consular Representation in British Hong Kong' *Pacific Affairs* vol. 71, no. 3, 2003: 359.
78 HKMS 158-1-283: 'HT Morgan (Commonwealth Office) to MacLehose (Foreign Office)' (23 May 1963), [2]. See chapter 3 where this is developed further.

3   1963

Introduction

The 'who, when and why' of the Hong Kong riot of 1956 in the colonial compensation scheme of 1957 demonstrated that its anatomy of rule-bound impartiality gave a false impression. On close inspection, the British produced a list of recipients who were approved commercial representatives of the KMT, who distinguished themselves by their political pliancy. The misleading nature of the British administration's frequent insistence that law and order principles were equally applied to KMT and communists alike was also revealed by lax policing of KMT militants using Hong Kong as a staging base for sabotage raids into China throughout the 1950s.

In 1963, a noticeable increase in American support for KMT special operations units operating in mainland China forced the British administration to tighten up its approach. It came under increasing pressure from the People's Republic to stop allowing misuse of the colony. This challenges a narrative of British law and order indifference that has dominated explanations of British policy in the Hong Kong historiography. The U.S. State Department used raids by Hong Kong-based KMT militants as a way to pinch China for transgressions elsewhere. The British used their suppression from 1963 onwards as a release valve from Chinese communist pressures.

The 1956 riot was ruled by the British colonial administration of Hong Kong to be a Chinese communist and KMT turf war. The communists in Hong Kong refuted any suggestion that they played an aggressive role in the riot. They strongly criticised the decision of colonial authorities not to pay them compensation despite heavy losses to individuals including farmers and textile workers, trade union officers and social welfare workers.[1] Their ongoing narrative that the British administration of Hong Kong aided and abetted the KMT in continuing sabotage raids on the mainland questioned whether the porous border policy necessarily implied policing the colony inadequately. In their account, the British administration lacked control over law and order in Hong Kong in 1956, resulting in the lives and interests of Chinese working people in the colony being damaged. In 1963, the British policy of pretending vigilance over the KMT violence changed abruptly into a policing action that stopped it from abusing the hospitality of the colony.

One could nominate the realities of the KMT by the early 1960s: dissolute in its external affairs purpose, isolated from historical destiny, using survivalism against memories of malfeasance, prone to weakening the American example by obliging their assistance on the sovereign soil of other nations, etc. Its anatomy, for whatever it was worth, had become a fanciful nationalism stronger in vengeance than transcendental unity. If inclined, one could read a KMT anatomy along these lines in this chapter. The anatomy is best left as an inference made by the reader from the actions that are described and the positions taken. The KMT has long touted Taiwan as what China might have been. By the 1960s, the exemplary anatomy – at least as far as it raised capacity for progress and the potentials of technological productivism – was a communist one, not the home ground of the reactionary bourgeois set as it had long been.

The apex of the relationship between the Kuomintang government of Taiwan and the U.S. State Department occurred in 1957–1958 when the Americans agreed to arm Taiwan with nuclear-capable Matador missiles possessing a range of 1,600 kilometres and significantly increased its military aid.[2] This raised serious concerns in the CCP leadership that Taiwan had developed an invasion capability that required China to have nuclear capability itself. In 1962, the third Taiwan Strait crisis erupted out of major military reinforcements in Taiwan and in China, and the imposition by Chiang Kai-shek of a domestic 'return to the mainland tax' in the rebel province.[3] Brugger characterised the tensions as a moment when the Kuomintang 'began to think of taking advantage of China's natural calamities'[4] presumably referring to the tail end of the Great Leap Forward. A meeting of U.S. and Chinese ambassadors in Warsaw in 1962 resulted in the assurance of the Kennedy administration to China that the United States would not back any attempted invasion attempt by the KMT.[5]

The policy of the British government in Hong Kong had until 1963 been conformable with the international tensions. In 1948, Governor Grantham had rebuffed the accusation of the administration's connivance with the KMT, pleading several spurious examples of not giving the KMT any accreditation in the public affairs of Hong Kong. The penultimate year of his ten-year premiership of Hong Kong was marred by the riot of 1956. The underwhelming recognition of the KMT in the lack of criminal reprisals after the riot could not have been more obvious to the communists. In 1963, however, the KMT received special regard from the colonial government's criminal trial system that it could have done well without. The

British narrative about the KMT had, by 1963, seldom seemed so much like it was rewriting history.

Beneath a rhetoric of non-recognition, or reasonable vigilance against republican militancy, a generally pro-KMT position of the colonial government existed in the years leading to 1963 when the release valve strategy came into play. The headline story of Hong Kong's post-war history was not that the colonial government played off the communists and the KMT against each other, or maintained strict ambivalence toward them both. It was that the colonial government held a tolerant position on the KMT militants for as long as it did, given the trouble that nearby China could have made. A discernible divide-and-rule position was applied by colonial authorities among militant and non-militant elements of the KMT, and it gained new momentum in 1963. It did not involve the communists. They had become seasonal allies of the British.

By 1963, what the KMT said it stood for, or not, had become an incidental question because of the consolidation of communist power in China. Chinese communism had no such question marks over its projection of an anatomy. Asserting technological control of the country, along with the purging and career-blocking, were communist responses to the tensions between 'Red thinking' and intellectualism that became a dominant issue in New China. How could a nation develop modernity in life when such a large part of the population was catching up on scientific thinking once represented entirely by Old Society forces? In this respect, there was an alignment of anatomy and practice in the communist tradition that was historically reliable and acute in its diagnosis. By making the advantages of modernity a futurist dream, champions of colonialism's comparable anatomy either knew it was fraudulent from the outset or repeated an abstraction of civilisation without sensing a need to investigate its truth.

The KMT had lost the fight over control of productive means in China, but its technological and business acumen had ready markets among the colonial enclaves. An influx of KMT capital and personnel escaped into South East Asia, Hong Kong and Taiwan hot and exhausted from a storm of retribution churning up the climes of China. The commercial windfall of the British colonial administration in the early 1950s contained the seeds of the 1956 riot, and this is why the situation in China in the early 1950s explains much. It was not only wealthy technocrats and businessmen, but violent rabble-rousers with unfinished business who poured over the border into the colony. The Chinese communist government told the British in Hong Kong who was coming, and that they were not always good news. The British ignored this advice until a historic about-face in 1963 so convincing that it even got the KMT-sponsoring Americans worried.

This chapter outlines a rash of prosecutions, imprisonments and deportations in Hong Kong against KMT agents in 1963. The British colonial administration denied that these activities were a result of closer diplomatic relations with the People's Republic. But it was also an occasional admission that the British were working on communist intelligence – details of which are revealed in this chapter. The relationship of the United States and the British colonial administration can be seen through the lens of American support for the KMT at a historical moment when the British decided that turning a blind eye to KMT sabotage activities on the mainland was no longer a plausibly deniable foreign policy position.

After the British actions in 1963 are described, the chapter gives details of the British wedge between the Chinese communists and the U.S. State Department by examining the world each wanted to create in its own image. This chapter contends that communist influence in British law and order priorities in Hong Kong grew throughout the late 1950s and early 1960s. The reasons for the raids and prosecutions against KMT militants, and the British admissions of working with the communist Chinese to give effect to them, are covered in the opening sections of this chapter. The increasing tensions between the Americans and the British in 1963 are covered in a subsequent chapter. In one case, a British official is quoted as saying that the more the U.S.-backed KMT anti-communism manifested itself, the less the British would have to deal with communists via Hong Kong.[6] This supports the thesis advanced earlier in the book that Whitehall, like a shuttlecock, had whipped back over the net like a backhand smash when it sacrificed KMT militants to Peking's demand in order to ease pressures in the East Asian region.

Why the crackdown began

The British colonial government became deeply enmeshed in the illegal activities of the post-civil war Kuomintang. On Naylor's account, the KMT's Shanghai incarnation, for example, was itself was little more than 'a merger of several triad style societies' led by Chiang Kai-shek.[7] In 1949, much of the underworld of Shanghai relocated to Hong Kong and some of the elders retired in Northern Burma. Although the KMT newcomers in Hong Kong had difficulty establishing themselves against local ethnic *chiu chau* gangsters, in the Shan states the KMT remnants thrived as they stepped in to control the opium trade after self-rule was granted to Burma, and, happily for the British, they did all their banking through Hong Kong.[8] The local *chiu chau* gangs found a lucrative role in the international trafficking of opium and heroin.[9] The KMT was, in Naylor's view, 'a confluence of anti-communist and organised-crime interests', and thus part of the economic fabric of British colonialism in the colony.[10]

Many factors explain the about-face of the British colonial administration on Hong Kong being used as a base for KMT sabotage runs. The geopolitics of 1963 witnessed increasingly frosty relations between Russia and China over whether the future of communism would be best achieved by engagement with the West or continued renunciation of capitalism. British Hong Kong could sidle up to communist China in a manner that did not acknowledge its revolutionary aim, but nevertheless saw a mutual advantage in easing pressures with symbolic measures. In 1962, urban food shortages prompted Beijing into a 'return to the village' program to make peasants return to their place of origin, known as *huixiang*.[11] This was at least in part responsible for a surge of around 15,000 people who crossed the Hong Kong border on an eased border policy in April 1962.[12] The British government subsequently rounded up and returned 60,000 people to Guangdong province, presumably after the crisis had passed.[13]

A further reason as to why, in 1963, the British revisited the KMT militancy question was local and pragmatic. The sensitivity of the colony to water shortages reached its peak. In 1964, British Hong Kong and the People's Republic signed an agreement to siphon a surplus 70,000 litres a day from China's East River. A reliable water supply was such a big political problem for colonial authorities that its solution was not necessarily inconsistent with jailing a group of KMT troublemakers that Peking had long resented remaining at large.

The British administration also doubtless calculated that Taiwan needed Hong Kong's trade dollars more than their intelligence agents. Over $50 million in foodstuffs including pigs, fruit and vegetables were imported from Taiwan, and the Colonial Secretary held a view that this was 'particularly important to us as an alternative source of food should for one reason or other supplies from China deteriorate or fail'.[14] Nevertheless, it was clear that the British had the KMT in Taipei in their pocket. The colonial administration was not fearful of a trade imbalance being used as a threat by Taipei because the Shan states opium trade, and its banking support through Hong Kong, were worth far more to the nationalists than agricultural exports.

Surprisingly little is known about the KMT operations in China that suddenly concerned the British in 1963. CIA reports usually relied on left-wing papers translated from Chinese in Hong Kong. They described KMT units of four or five men who stashed arms and explosives on Hong Kong's outer islands before entering the colony. They took motorised junks to various destinations in the mainland parts of the Pearl River Delta, via their weapons stash. They were often poorly trained. Mainland Chinese newspapers boasted high detection and elimination rates.

Nationalist newspapers in Taiwan claimed the KMT had landed eight units in China in April 1963, and that seven of these were successful in their sabotage missions.[15] The communist papers promptly reported that six groups of armed agents were 'wiped out'.[16] Common sabotage targets included rail lines, railway stations and telegraph wires. Saboteurs routinely used American-supplied detonators and ordinance. On some occasions, they would bring from Hong Kong medicines that were exchanged with villagers for housing or other assistance. In such cases, they planned stay two or three months although in his report to the Secretary of State for the Commonwealth, Governor Robert Black ventured a view that 'they seemed to have little idea of what this would involve'.[17]

The modus operandi of the KMT in China changed quite a bit over the years from 1950 to 1963. In the early years, as one intercepted communist report framed it, 'a good deal of the dirty work is done by agents worming their way into Communist Party organisations'.[18] KMT-affiliated squads went from operations based in China, including raiding public warehouses, inciting locals to refrain from paying the grain levy and opportunistic assassination of local communist security force members, to hit-and-run tactics using Hong Kong or Macau as bases, or forming sleeper cells embedded in the villages on the pretext of sons returning to help with the harvest or see their mothers, before making their attacks and hopefully vanishing to safety across the border.

The raids

In February or March 1963, the CCP shared 'evidence' with the British colonial authorities in Hong Kong of a 'K.M.T. plot to organise sabotage and assassinations on a large scale in both in China and in Hong Kong and Macau'.[19] The first indications of a major British offensive against the KMT on Hong Kong soil came in May and June 1963. Hong Kong's police were said in one report to have arrested several members of a 'highly organised espionage and sabotage ring operating inside the colony on behalf of the Chinese Nationalist government' in response to the 'eight unit raid' a month earlier.[20] The level of expertise of KMT operatives should be doubted; the Governor himself wrote about most such men being ex-army KMT whose leader 'was given about two hours of training in sabotage work and the others even less'.[21] The press report continued by explaining that more than seventy members of Special Branch took part in a series of raids that were 'the biggest ever undertaken in the Colony'.[22]

Along with several agents, the haul included secret documents, codes, radio equipment and a poorly concealed list of nationalist intelligence agents living locally. Two of the agents caught were in a downtown import-export firm, and one of them was said to be a high-ranking officer in the Kuomintang Intelligence Service (KIS). The media attitude toward the KMT had moved from indifference to contextualising a new enemy. It was reported that the demeanour of these KMT agents 'has become increasingly arrogant'.[23]

Operations were mounted in the colony on 29 June 1963 against KIS and sabotage groups operating in the colony. By mid-July, there were detained by the authorities some forty-nine people, and of these, fourteen were released for lack of evidence, leaving thirty-five to answer further questions.[24] The security forces had captured leaders of an Intelligence Bureau Unit and a KIS 2nd Section Unit, both of whom were claimed by Special Branch 'to be operating against the Mainland from Hong Kong'.[25] Also captured were two very senior members of the KMT Investigation Unit, along with explosives, incendiary devices, a radio station capable of reaching Taiwan, frontier passes and a Chinese communist army uniform.

The prosecutions

There had been repeated, and denied, complaints by the Chinese communists in 1956–1957 that the British administration of Hong Kong was passively or actively assisting KMT terror raids on the mainland by the looseness of their policing in the colony. Yet this is what a sentencing judge had to say in 1963 when putting away for ten years a Hau Sang factory worker for possession of detonators and timing pencils:

> It was common knowledge that in recent months Hong Kong had been used by certain individuals, alleged to be saboteurs, working against the interests of a nation with which HMG has diplomatic relations. Explosives could have been used by saboteurs whose acts would upset public tranquillity and might even endanger the good relations of the State itself with its neighbours. Cases of this sort called for deterrent and exemplary sentences.[26]

For a judicial officer of British Hong Kong to more than imply that, in 1963, the use of the colony as a staging post for KMT terrorism in mainland China was recent could only be called an obvious departure from the truth, if not a surprising one. Presumably more galling to the Chinese communists was a report claiming to be a news item that the United States had assisted Taiwan to set up 7,000-strong special operations units to operate in China; they too were reported to be 'working through Hong Kong in recent months'.[27] More notably raising eyebrows in this period, however, was the suggestion in 1963 from Murray MacLehose, at that time in the Foreign Office, that the Formosans (Taiwanese) be denied transit and migration to British territory, including Hong Kong, 'as a means of exerting pressure on the Nationalist authorities if they continue to mount subversive and sabotage activities from Hong Kong'.[28] This suggestion was dressed down quickly by Hong Kong authorities and British immigration on grounds of the media furore it would cause. It gave no clue that MacLehose would become one of Hong Kong's most assured hands as Governor.

The British prosecutions commenced with Mr Chau Mau Lam. After changing his plea from 'not guilty' to 'guilty', he was sentenced to ten years' imprisonment for illegal possession of arms and ten years for illegal possession of explosives.[29] This was the first of a series of open-and-shut prosecutions. In much the same form as current anti-terror offences in Western countries, the law of the colony had been amended in 1950 to cover anyone with intent to cause an explosion with an explosive substance, or conspired to do so, or aided or abetted anyone intending to do so by providing money or premises.[30] Therefore, knowledge of a bomb-maker's whereabouts or association with one could be quite enough to land an individual in prison for a lengthy stint. The local media did its best to give an impression that the KMT had outstayed its welcome in Hong Kong; one report complained that the last group of deported Formosans had falsely accused the Hong Kong police of mistreating them despite the force's 'rigorous orders to maintain the colony's strict neutrality in the Chinese communist-Nationalist conflict'.[31]

As Chau Mau Lam pleaded guilty at the last moment, he was allowed to serve his sentences concurrently. In a separate case, KMT agent Li Chi Tai received the same sentences for the same offences that Chau Mau Lam did, but had another two years added to his sentence for possessing counterfeit communist currency – somewhat corroborating the earlier-reported communist suspicion about economic crimes undermining its political control on the mainland. Yet one should not take from this any suggestion that the British practices of prosecution and imprisonment of KMT agents were just or fair. Long terms of imprisonment for agents had been, in 1963, a new order replacing an earlier practice of detaining agents for questioning then deporting them back to Formosa.[32] More questionably, the colonial authorities suspended habeas corpus on nationalist spies. An official in the Colonial Office noted to one in the Hong Kong Special Branch:

> the Governor has advanced good reasons why save in a few cases it is impractical to prosecute. At the same time he made the point that

there were some of these saboteurs for who we could not possibly contemplate deportation back to Formosa because of their importance in the KMT organisation and the information they possess. He made proposals for holding such persons in detention indefinitely, without trial.[33]

Governor Black could not make up his mind whether some of the KMT agents in the government's custody were rank amateurs or espionage veterans. Some of them knew too much about the British or American modus in Hong Kong to be allowed to fall into communist clutches. There were thirty-five suspects initially detained for further questioning; one was prosecuted for illegal possession of a radio transmitting set, four were prosecuted for arms and explosives possession, and thirty were deported back to Taiwan, at least according to the official position.[34]

Whether because of their arrogance or possession of sensitive information, some of the arrested KMT agents were clearly earmarked to avoid trial and rot on remand indefinitely. These shadow inmates raised not only a question about how the information was to be attained from them, but what sensitive information about communist China they had that the British could use to parlay favour with the Americans, or what information they had gathered about the British. By 1963, the foothills of Kowloon had all the installations of a receiving station of global importance in the grand game of intelligence in Central and East Asia. Local human intelligence was another contribution that Hong Kong could make to the Americans as China pursued and entered the nuclear age, and fomented communist uprisings in other countries.

British admissions

The events of 1963 formed a communist story of Hong Kong, not a colonial one, and communist influence in the affairs of Hong Kong has been ignored in the history parsed by the West. The theory of British impartiality in Hong Kong has enjoyed a starring role in the historiography dating from 1949 and was most recently repeated by Tsang, who recorded that communists and Kuomintang were equally welcome to call Hong Kong home 'provided that they obeyed the law and did not engage in activities detrimental to relations between British and Chinese governments'.[35]

Such as it is, the accepted history of events in Hong Kong in 1963 credits the Labour opposition in the House of Commons led by Harold Wilson for prevailing on the Macmillan government to request the Americans talk with 'bandit' KMT forces to stop their campaign of letter bombing targets in China, bombing communists in Hong Kong and sending sabotage raids over the border.[36] This bipartisanism, so says Lombardo, was why the British administration in Hong Kong felt licensed to prosecute and imprison KMT agents rather than deport them to Taiwan.[37] In itself, this is a good example of the questionable narrative that the British and Americans uneasily worked together and the British, as ever, were the ones who took the initiative in matters of foreign affairs when something morally repugnant was discovered within their bailiwick. Another version of the events of 1963 can be told without entirely upbraiding the standard history because the British response to KMT cross-border and Hong Kong terrorism in 1963 was largely symbolic, if not without its value to Peking, which was reputedly upset that the U.S. Consulate in the colony had grown to be the biggest American outpost in the world. In the face of that, any kind of British symbolism in the form of subduing the CCP's old nationalist foe would presumably do.

In 1963, the pro-KMT press accused the British colonial administration of Hong Kong of being a glove puppet of Chinese communism, and the British agreed. *The Express* reported that the Chinese communists 'brought pressure on Whitehall to instruct Hong Kong authorities to stamp out KMT intelligence activities by the end [of June 1963] and provided lists of KMT agents'.[38] To this Governor Black sheepishly responded:

> in view of undesirability of revealing that the CPG [Chinese People's Government] have pressed us on this or furnished names there should be issued a reminder of the stated position of the government in the home parliament on the KMT and the explosives that had been found in Hong Kong.[39]

H.T. Morgan in the Commonwealth Office was quite candid about the relationship of the British to the communist Chinese:

> But we have in the past asked the Chinese for information and now that we have got it we should be prepared to make the most of it and let them see we have done so. If we did anything to let the Chinese think that we feel answerable to them we should be inviting perpetual Chinese pressure. But the fact surely is that over Hong Kong we are already under perpetual Chinese pressure and the way to minimise it is to take effective action against activities which we ourselves deplore.[40]

It was understandable that, after having come down in the world after the Second World War, the government circles of British of Hong Kong and the Commonwealth Office retained some sensitivity about being told what to do by the Chinese communist government. The British authorities in

Hong Kong had grown accustomed over a century not only to a free hand from HMG (Her Majesty's Government) under a policy of Indirect Rule, but also to dealing obliquely with warlords or gangsters over the border on matters of mutual concern.

After 1949, the communists had arrived in power. The British encountered an organised central government with a sound intelligence of its enemies lurking on British soil. Hong Kong authorities had to contemplate taking their orders from two masters while pretending that the brutish communists were merely staking out a course of action that the colonial government had wit enough to enact itself. In response to a suggested plan by MacLehose to limit Chinese Nationalist immigration to the United Kingdom, the Chief Secretary in Hong Kong observed candidly to the Commonwealth Office:

> Doubt whether pressure along these lines would in itself be sufficient to deter KMT from using Hong Kong as a base for anti-CPG activities if they are determined to go on doing this. If action demonstrably came from HMG it would do us some good with the CPG by demonstrating that we are in earnest in trying to suppress KMT activities here.[41]

After more than a century of imperial meddling in the affairs of China, the communists must have enjoyed treating the colonial outpost as a junior functionary whose adventurous conceits had been brought into line by Whitehall. In early May 1963, the Chinese Ministry of Foreign Affairs advised the British Charge D'Affairs in Peking that 'they had evidence of a K.M.T plot to organise sabotage and assassinations on a large scale in both China and in Hong Kong and Macau'.[42] Regarding this as credible, the British had to act in Hong Kong promptly to appease the communists. By now, policy had become all about buying breathing space. There was a Burmese saying that 'when China spits, Burma swims'. British Hong Kong was, by 1963, firmly ensconced in a lifebuoy.

Although their views were routinely ignored, it remains wise not to believe everything Chinese communists remember about the past. For them, history is a recitation produced by a committee meeting and disseminated in an approved training manual by carefully selected cadres whose fates ride on success in indoctrinating the upcoming generation. Chinese Marxists refer to their 'achievements in historiography' and their 'dominance in historical studies'[43] in the tone that Western liberals reserve for a title-winning basketball team. That is, revisionist bourgeois history readings continue to claim they are open to competition with other viewpoints despite being quite faultless compared to other readings. There is nothing equivocal about a Sino-Marxist's belief about their triumph over all other readings of history. That is what they know and feel. The great fool's paradise of the larger historiography lays in both sides pretending the debate is open, whilst holding fervently to a view that only one is unexceptionable. This intractable quality makes impossible a suggestion, for instance, that the British colonial government had been amenable to communist Chinese cooperation on the KMT issue from 1956 but only acted on record in 1963. The documentary support for this comes from Lennox-Boyd's comment to Grantham in October 1956:

> you should ask for full details [of those who] perpetuate outrages there . . . you should ask for full details of the persons concerned and evidence of their intentions.[44]

In its context, this neither has the quality of asking the communists for something the British already knew nor a pretence of interest in receiving information. It would seem to be either a request for information the British knew the communists could not give at that point, or an early example of British-Sino partnership, or an intention to develop one.

The Hyatt Americans

The KMT increasingly became a liability to the U.S. State Department in the early 1960s. The problem with America's lobby lounge influence in southern China was that the KMT as its proxy had only one objective – futile revenge – and no country to call its own in mainland Asia. The KMT had no choice but to meddle in the business of third-party sovereign states in diaspora pockets or old colonies to fund and execute its harassment of mainland China. Taipei was adventurous beyond its abilities. From a comfortable distance, when bad news broke, the Americans told the KMT when and where to stop their activities. But they seldom told them when to go. The power of when and where to initiate subversive actions lay in 1963 with a handful of hard-line Taipei hierarchs and the watery-eyed Chiang Kai-shek – who by then was 75 years old. The KMT leadership had become frail and erratic at a point in time when coherent anti-communist movements across Asia should have been doing well.

Although Sino-American meetings occurred occasionally at the ambassadorial level, the Americans sought cantonment from the communist Chinese by choosing not to have official diplomatic relations with them. This made the CIA reliant on British Hong Kong and Portuguese Macau, as well as translations of newspapers inside and outside of China. The KMT operated in a free space allowed by the Americans until such time as it created a diplomatic incident with a third nation that was undesirable from a U.S. perspective. The U.S. anti-communist policy of the 1960s left it battling too many foes on too many fronts. The Americans opted to contract out their responsibilities to whoever would take their money, hold a gun and sound like an ally. From the heavy commitment of the United States to Vietnam and Korea as hot sites of the Cold War, it can be inferred that other locations of friction assumed a lower priority. The Americans contented themselves with using local proxies to influence balances in favour of reformist colonialism, standover warlordism or pliant presidential democracy as convenience demanded.

Some American intelligence operatives went to superb lengths to understand the psyche of Chinese communists.[45] However, due to their diplomatic disconnection with China, they relied in southern China on supposition with second-hand news, sometimes making them little better informed than journalists bandying about ideas for comment pieces in an R&R town. This was an example of an intelligence update in the style of scribblings made on the back of a drinks coaster:

> In all probability the Kuomintang in Thailand will not 'fight' the Communists. There will be a gradual shift in sentiment in the Chinese community toward the communist regime in China. Once the Communists really set up their government the Chinese in Thailand will jump on the bandwagon.[46]

Set against slack journalism were surprisingly good CIA capabilities on anything to do with Chinese military capacity during the Korean War era. One report gave precise details on political officers being sent to the Kwangtung River Defence Command to assist in the poor morale of its soldiers, Chinese communist submarine operations with the Russians out of Port Arthur and the capabilities of gunboats in Shanghai.[47] This quality of intelligence could only be derived from KMT sleeper agents with radios. Although nothing in CIA records attests to a working relationship whereby the Americans exchanged intelligence from KMT deep cover agents in the north for training and guns for their southern China raids out of Hong Kong, it is difficult to see why such reciprocities would be thought unlikely.

On the issue of Hong Kong, the British government in Whitehall, along with its marionette administration in Hong Kong, was sandwiched between the People's Republic of China and the United States. The KMT in Hong Kong was resourced and trained well by the Americans in Taipei and perhaps a little too eager to fight the communists. Throughout the early 1960s, the United States stepped up its support for KMT agents visiting China to conduct espionage and sabotage activities. The Americans also gave particular support to KMT irregular troops in the borderlands of Southern Yunnan in 1960–1961 during a joint Chinese communist and Burmese offensive against them in that period.[48] The KMT in Thailand did not melt into the arms of the communists, but became an unorthodox source of foreign exchange for the hierarchs of Taipei. Nationalist Chinese troops sustained themselves through control of a major opium smuggling route running from Burma to northern Thailand to Taiwan by plane and then to the United States that was still operational in 1971.[49] This northern Thailand KMT organisation was referred to in one U.S. press report as 'an opium army subsidised by the Nationalist Chinese',[50] even if it had, in fact, become one of many gangster KMT jungle militias with illicit activities subsidising Taipei.

The KMT liability in regional politics

The British in Hong Kong were put between a rock and a hard place by China and the United States due to their policy on KMT activities in southeastern China. As the imperial mantle passed to the Americans, on the southern border of China with Burma they came under increasing pressure for supporting KMT pockets in Burma not only indirectly from China, but Burma itself and the episode raised a lesson in sovereignty. One U.S. media report concerned the neutral Burmese government which accused the United States of 'a grossly unfriendly act' in 'permitting' the KMT in Formosa to deliver U.S. arms via U.S. planes into Shan state to 'an outlaw group of Nationalist Chinese (KMT) soldiers holed up [there].'[51]

The misuse of Burma's territory 'acutely embarrassed' its government.[52] The Burmese were plying both the United States and China for foreign aid. Yet there can be no doubt that 'Formosa's purpose of maintaining the KMT troops undoubtedly has been to harass the Communist mainland from its Southern border'.[53] This made U.S. choices about its Burma policy difficult. The neutrality and non-interventionism of Burma mattered to the United States in an era when the so-called Domino Theory still held sway.

The British sponsorship of the KMT in southern China from Hong Kong after 1950 was an example of an imperial power allowing its sovereign state to be used to interfere in the affairs of another sovereign state. The Americans backing the KMT in Burma was an episode of them using Burma as if it was their sovereign state in order to attack another sovereign state. Even the Americans at the height of their power had to admit to the undesirable Westphalian amendment implied by that position. It was easier on historical principle to carry on in ambiguity like the British, even after their bluff was called.

The expatriate KMT forces had a role to play for U.S. Secretary of State Dean Rusk in southeastern China but not on the Burmese border: 'the toughest US message to Chiang Kai-shek was quickly dispatched to Formosa, and the quickest compliance in memory followed.'[54] The British self-interest came to the fore during such episodes, with their official H.T. Morgan opining:

> the American angle is a difficult one but there again the more effectively the Americans be made to speak up in Taipeh the less need there will be for us to traffick with the Communists.[55]

Nevertheless, although the airstrip in Burma had been closed down, the Americans did not retract from indirectly supporting the KMT in their dispersion points in northern Burma, Laos and northern Thailand by applying next to no pressure on the opium issue. The United States also got quite testy with the Burmese for doing nothing when Chinese communist troops assisting them in a friendly border demarcation exercise went a little further south than anticipated to take the opportunity to rough up a number of KMT encampments. The Americans were not surprised; their intelligence was sound. They knew since late 1960 of a secret agreement between Burma and China for each party to operate against Chinese nationalist troops up to 15 miles inside each other's border.[56]

By wargaming the sprawling tableau of the Cold War, the Americans learned one thing: Chiang Kai-shek would never return to mainland China to rule, but having any anti-communist ally in South East Asia was better than fighting battles with no coalition. The imperious days of the British in Hong Kong had now past and left-over colonies were conduits of a constrained geopolitics that aimed at hanging on to economic enclaves and places where colonial power had historically accreted. Having perused a translation of the *People's Daily* in July 1963, H.M. Consul, Peking, advised of its report that 'thirty-one armed United States-Chiang agents' had been killed or captured in Kwuntung since the beginning of June 1963.[57] This came after the success in the previous year when nine groups had been 'annihilated' and could be counted as 'another great victory for the army of the coastal area'.[58]

When one does not necessarily trust the truth of a newspaper claim, ample faith can nevertheless be given to what the writer was trying to say, or at the audience at which their influence was aimed. The unambiguous designation in 1963 of the KMT agents as American-trained could not be called a watershed in Chinese communist propaganda. Until around then, however, the reference to the work of fiendish work of 'imperialists' was by far the most common.

The relationship between the British in Whitehall and the U.S. State Department became fraught in 1963. The British had adopted an anti-KMT militant stance in 1963, but wanted to portray their position as business as usual. MacLehose in the Foreign Office made several approaches to the Americans 'about KMT intentions' which had ended in apparent confusion between the parties and, as Chief Secretary Willan remarked, 'the possibilities of misunderstanding and misinterpretation over this wretched business seem limitless: I wonder sometimes whether any of it is deliberate'.[59] The British intended for their crackdown to be a short-term appeasement of the Chinese communists, but the Americans treated it as a literal change in British policy and the British responded, as only they could, with mild incredulity that they were taken as shutting down CIA-sponsored sabotage operations in southern China. Yet the simpering of the British toward communists on information about KMT targets in Hong Kong could not be merely in the imagination of the Americans. In the vernacular of the schoolyard, the British expected mercy from the school bully because the joke they told about him was really quite funny.

A couple of British Members of Parliament (MPs) had an instructive exchange of correspondence over the American-British rift over the KMT in 1963. Philip Noel-Baker, the Secretary of State for the Commonwealth in the late 1940s, was pleased that the U.S. State Department had been made aware of statements made by the government in Parliament concerning the KMT mayhem in southern China. In a letter to Nigel Fisher, the responsible minister for the Commonwealth in 1963, he observed that if Kennedy and Rusk would tell Chiang Kai-shek to stop the raids 'they would unquestionably stop; and I cannot doubt that they ought to do so'.[60] He further opined that:

> The raids amount to no more than indiscriminate murder of innocent Chinese civilians on the mainland. Their only political effect is to solidify the support of the Chinese people for the Government of Peking; as a means of making anybody believe that Chiang Kai-shek will someday be able to invade China, they are ludicrously inadequate.[61]

After all, the British were no longer observing, as they did in 1950–1952, a southern China beset by an intelligence war, banditry, skirmishes, and county-level KMT military resistance to the communist rule of the country. The KMT liked, even in the early 1960s, to refer to the communist 'rebellion' on the mainland and itself as the true party of government awaiting its imminent return. Once that manner of thinking passed into fantasy, much in British regard for the legitimacy of KMT anti-communist violence inside their colony and on the mainland had to be adjusted rather coldly.

In 1950, 150 pro-Peking trade unionists rioted against 1,500 former KMT soldiers in a refugee camp on Mt Davis, Hong Kong Island; in response, the British sent the soldiers to a settlement at Rennie's Mill, a remote part of East Kowloon.[62] After the riot of 1956, the constant refrain of the communists was that KMT agents charged with murder were being let off scot-free.[63] There does seem to be a moderate response by the colonial government to the KMT's involvement in the Double Ten riots. Although it was not without a history, it was without a future.

History of KMT enemy status

The decline of the KMT outside of Taiwan was not due only to the tensions they created with the U.S. State Department. Their history with the British was more like toleration or joint venturing than love. The policing of the KMT in Hong Kong was a deft combination of management of business opportunities by the British and, in good time, making an example of extremist KMT post-civil war remnants by imprisoning them in 1963. Governor Grantham had nominated a figure of straw in 1948 when he said that: 'the KMT is always ready to edge its way in and try to establish its authority in the colony'.[64] Before 1963, the questions for the British administration were: which factions of the KMT should have influence and what criteria were best in identifying such factions? After 1963, the question was: how much control of the KMT off-scourings would satisfy Peking?

There were three sources of power in the economy and political life of British Hong Kong in the years between 1950 and 1963: the government (including its local colonial and Whitehall grandees, the civil service and the gangland-managing Special Branch), the Chinese communists (including their unflinching local proxies in trade unions, social welfare organisations and assassination groups) and the Kuomintang, made up as it was of a wide range of elements ranging from extremist ex-military agents, businessmen and a variety of political members of a dizzying array of cliques and societies from the defunct Nationalist regime. How did the new British approach to the KMT in 1963 relate to past treatment?

Over a period of one hundred years, the colonial government of Hong Kong had a purported policy of viewing triad members as 'inconsistent with the maintenance of good rule and constituted authority'.[65] After the Second World War, such an approach, if it had ever really held, descended into disaccreditation of gangster factions deemed no longer to have anything to offer the British administration by way of reliable commercial partnership. In 1946, the Kuomintang government in Nanking was recognised by Whitehall as the national government of China. Yet the local branch of the KMT in Hong Kong was thought in colonial circles not to be actually representing Nanking in the years immediately following the Second World War. The KMT offices in the colony were raided by the returning British authorities in September 1945. They alleged that documents had been found to 'indicate' that the local KMT had no credentials from the Chungking government (as it then was).[66]

The returning British administration accused local KMT operatives of conducting an unauthorised 'ferreting out' of those who had collaborated with the Japanese regime to extort money from them.[67] Local KMT leader Shun Chit-son was arrested, warned against 'usurping the functions of the Hong Kong police' and released.[68] British state intelligence officer in Hong Kong Harold Little (MI5) recommended:

> signal to Chungking should emphasise that police raid had nothing to do with the political side but was carried out on the basis of violations of the law which applies equally to all in this colony.[69]

This was how the British administration manifested its charade in Hong Kong that the KMT and the communists would be treated the same. The British Mandarinate in Hong Kong liked to claim that its modus operandi was not to disturb the political position of the KMT by local actions unnecessarily, and this was thought to be especially important in the years leading up to their loss of the civil war. The colonial government's only real interest was in channelling the KMT's twilight booty by insisting that its bearers *not* be involved colonial politics. This did not bring to an end communist and KMT tit-for-tat violence against each other in the colony after the civil war ended. The most obvious incarnation of the nationalist commercial license, Hong Kong-based funding of KMT groups prosecuting violence in post-civil war southern China, also continued to be an unspoken topic throughout the 1950s. The open border policy of the British colonial government toward Chinese political refugees, and its refusal to police those who left the colony for China of their own free will, placed KMT radicalism in resistance to the communist regime low on the British agenda. The risks posed by KMT political agents meddling in Hong Kong's dockside trade unions, education and political life were significantly higher on the colonial agenda.

In the case of Shum Chit-son, the British administration had an early opportunity to realise a need to sharpen up its intelligence act. Yet it transpired that in Chungking, the KMT officer responsible for Hong Kong, General Wu Teh Chen, when alerted to the 'over-enthusiastic activities' of local KMT and Youthful Corps operatives, said he would instruct Shum to curb his activities and that he planned to send a new representative who 'would have instructions to cooperate fully with the new administration'.[70] When one of Hong Kong's intelligence officers learned of this, he described it as 'very embarrassing';[71] i.e. Shum was not an opportunistic gangster, he *was* the KMT's chief operative in Hong Kong, even if the KMT recognised that by replacing him his activities had breached, in diplomatic terms, the fatuous protocol of the British administration against overtly political behaviour in their colony. Shum was another KMT member who over the years the British administration would designate as 'the wrong sort of KMT'.

There developed some subtlety about the colonial government's approach to the KMT in Hong Kong after the Second World War. In 1948, the quite recently installed Governor Grantham recorded in a memo to Arthur Creech Jones (a British MP at that time) that he had 'refrained studiously from doing anything that would give the Kuomintang "face" in the eyes of the Chinese population'.[72] This policy went to the symbolic extent of stopping national KMT elections in 1948 from occurring in Hong Kong to elect a local representative, although the election was not impeded in Macau. This frustration could not have offended the Central Committee in Nanking greatly, because it was busy retiring existing members from their seats in the rubber stamp parliament and replacing them *en bloc* with new blood from the Social Democrat Party and Young China Party.

No matter the apparently reformist trend, Grantham intoned to the Secretary of State for Commonwealth: 'the Kuomintang in Hong Kong has no official status, and its members are not invited to any official functions'.[73] By taking a theoretical position on recognition, the colonial government could maintain denials about the support of KMT violence by letting Hong Kong be used as a staging post, and maintain an undisclosed policy of preference in riot compensation for the right sort of KMT business people. The colonial government dealt with individual KMT members in a deeply patterned way rather than officially recognise their political party.

In June 1948, the KMT office holders attending British receptions in Hong Kong or actively house hunting in the colony constituted a near-'Who's Who' of the party. Despite Governor Grantham's protestation that no KMT representatives were 'given face' by the colonial administration,[74] he subsequently bragged about his invitees. The champagne sippers included General Chang Chun, Dr Sun Fo, Dr TV Soong, General Lun Yun, Ho Ying-chin, General Chang Fa Kuei, Dr Wang Shih-chieh – the Foreign Minister – and General Wei Li-Hung, the last Nationalist commander in Manchuria.[75] Among the confirmed house hunters in the colony were Mr T.W. Kwok, Mr Li Tai-chiu, Mr Li Ta Chau, General Wu and Chang Pao-shu, a former Secretary-General of the Kuomintang.[76]

Relentless testing at the margins of British authority by the KMT in Hong Kong made the government-to-government relationship prone to pitfalls. It was not viable colonial policy having to second-guess the KMT's innumerable factions, among them the New Guangxi Clique, the CC Clique, Yang Yongtai's Politics Research Group and the Whampoa Academy Clique. Instead, from the early to mid-1950s, the colony pursued a policy of equanimity allowing commercial scope to preferred KMT and tolerable communist operatives to conduct business.

The unfortunate turn of the colony toward the KMT in the riot response of 1956–1957 needs further little explanation. The contestation of the colony had been bubbling along in two naively ignored fora: (1) a vigorous assassination culture that thrived between the political extremes in the colony and (2) the controversial use of Hong Kong by the KMT as a staging post for reprisal raids on Chinese soil. British Hong Kong's policy of ignoring political violence it gained no advantage from regulating could not prevail indefinitely because American and communist Chinese support was needed equally, if at different times. It was a matter of keeping the door open.

The British colonial government had long recognised that in newspapers, stevedoring, manufacturing industry and finance in Hong Kong, the KMT held an unavoidable commercial dominance. The Chinese Manufacturers' Association had a Hong Kong Branch that simpered after the British; the organisation was headed in Canton by Mo Hing Cheung who was brother-in-law of Chiang Kai-Shek. The manufacturers were 'closely allied' with the Chinese Chamber of Commerce, Hong Kong, which 'traditionally supported' the Nanking government.[77] Although the colonial government was keen to appear to curb political influence of KMT factions in the colony, this did not prevent it from 'playing winners' among them, or ignoring KMT political violence across the border.

Unlike the communists, after 1949 the KMT did not, for its own reasons, seek official recognition from the British administration in Hong Kong. The apparent homogeneity of the population was no impediment for the British to identify Chinese Nationalist political extremists, or to refrain from their prosecution until necessary. Nor could it be said they had trouble distinguishing between those indulging in activities of the local business elite in support of sabotage committed across the border in China. The colonials simply needed to ask for communist help.

Conduct of colonial public policy in Hong Kong occurred through identifiable policies of discretion applied to individuals as much as through recognition governments offering assistance to their citizens in the colony. Policing restraint, when used in favour of KMT militants, fortified Anglo-American bonds. The first priority of every colonial administration in the colony was to require amenable KMT or communist operatives to mute their political loyalties as the price to pay for access to commercial opportunities in the colony. That British administrations turned a blind eye to the colony being used as a base for anti-communist insurgency operations during the 1950s suggests that the military license of the KMT to operate across the border was not part of the supposedly indifferent balance struck by the British and it gives quite a different – and much more biased – complexion to the local political ecosystem than the naïve literature of indifference can bring itself to recognise.

Exempting the KMT commercial license from a requirement of refraining from militant activism across the border seemed at odds with recognition of the People's Government. It originated in the British authorities not being able to beat the KMT and so electing to join them instead. Much of the leniency of the colonial government by the post-war years toward triad organisations dated from their unpleasant experience in dealing with Dr Sun Yat Sen. He had an order of banishment placed on him by the Colonial Secretary Lockhart in 1896 because of his 'plots and dangerous conspiracies against a neighbouring Empire'.[78] This position, by way of protest, resulted in the establishment of a new Hong Kong-based, pro-Sun triad network, the Chung Wo Tong.[79] After the KMT triumph in 1912, it became the genitor of several Wo societies including Wo Shing Wo, easily the most powerful triad organisation in Hong Kong by 1952.[80] The proliferation of underworld societies raised a serious question about how business was to occur in the colony.

Conclusion

The Chinese communists framed the public safety discourse of Hong Kong in the mid- to late 1950s but get no credit for it, so there can be little surprise that what happened in 1963 can likewise find no place in Hong Kong's history, and certainly not be recalled as a final friendly warning against Rightist activity in the colony before the tragedy of 1967. It would be factually acceptable simply to say that Whitehall muddled along between the Chinese communists and the Americans in Hong Kong, but that would lack the appeal of sounding principled as the colonial impartiality thesis falsely maintains.

Once understood, one can only read the dramatic distancing by Hong Kong authorities from the KMT in 1963, and its implication for British foreign policy in post-war East Asia as a short yet symbolic partnership with the communists, although any disavowal of the KMT or a radical change in course would affect the division of longstanding proceeds of various criminal enterprises from which the colonial government took benefit. That did not make British symbolism unimportant to the communist Chinese or the newest imperialists, the Americans. If one wished to file the events of 1963 under a label, 'pragmatic symbolism' would do well enough.

British Cold War policy shifted constantly in Hong Kong in the years between 1957 (the disavowal of communist compensation riot claims) and 1963 (the CCP giving the British a hit list of KMT agents in their colony). British official H.T. Morgan, with no shortage of candour, offered a view that 'the Chinese [communists] will be more interested in what we do than what we say' and that 'I should doubt whether the Chinese would on principle want any regular collaboration with us on a matter involving intelligence etc'.[81] This attitude signalled that the British were happy to make opportunist use of scraps that fell off the communist Chinese intelligence table and that, finally, it had registered that symbolic action was the best policy even if it strained the American friendship.

The frequent accusation made by the Chinese communists in 1956–1957 was that the British administration's compensation arrangements failed in their responsibility of working Chinese people in the colony. It only pretended to care. An odd line for communists to take, one might think, on refugee Rightists. The communists maintained that they had a mandate to protect common people from law and order breaches occurring under colonial rule. This could be laughed off by the British in 1957 without them taking steps to put the situation right, and that was exactly what they did. In 1963, however, the British were put to another sincerity test by the government in Peking. That it resulted in a rift between the British and the Americans over KMT terror raids inside southern China was evidence that British principles, at last, could at least momentarily transcend a Hong Kong colonial mindset of obsessively minding one's own business, or playing deputy sheriff to the Americans.

Violent acts – both in the form of the 1956 Hong Kong riots, and often abortive KMT sabotage raids on southern China via Macau or Hong Kong – were reminiscences. Those doing the violence, however, were too lost in a feeling that they acted as a vital force to realise that they were nihilists. They simply pulsed along like woozy jazz; propelled by old fervour and a disbelief in death's constraint. In this light, the riot of 1956 and the sabotage raids around Canton can be read as an example of indeterminate violence aimed at no realistic purpose, or violence as a refusal to accept one's founding political claims was dead. Amateurish KMT violence in Hong Kong and southern China in 1963 assumed sudden importance to Hong Kong's government. The comfortable British strategy of pairing commercial pacification with law and order laxity ended in 1963. The British missed their chance to disaggregate the factors of violence in 1956. They were too enmeshed themselves in protecting partners living the KMT thug life.

The British action on KMT nihilism in 1963 came thirteen years after the Chinese communist diagnosis of it. But it died hard among the Taiwanese nationalists and their American allies. For the British, although the KMT's raiding in China had been hopeless and largely harmless to their colony, it could be ignored for the sake of the Americans. In 1963, their relationship with the Chinese communists became epistemic for them in a way that it continued not to be for the KMT and the Americans. My general argument, raised in the opening chapter, is that British de facto support for the KMT's mainland violence caused it not to be a nullity.

The role of the British colonial government as a state sponsor of terrorism in China became unavailable in 1963 and, in any case, sat poorly with its desired image of a placeholder colonial power looking to get out of the game after dispatching a few more cargo pallets for posterity's sake. This intermediate position had disappeared in many places throughout the fast-failing 1960s empire. Only by inhabiting it could the revisionism of British moral superiority through the emerging human rights discourse become plausible. In the final chapter, a comparison is offered of British colonials and the communists by assessing how they acted towards intellectualism. My argument is that every ideological anatomy was an intellectual representation about modernity and who received an owner's share of it. The job of the next chapter, however, is to summarise the three major Cold War anatomies of southern China.

Notes

1 HKRS163-1-2029 (523/57/58): 'Communist Accounts': 'HK & Kowloon Spinning, Weaving and Dyeing Trade Workers General Union' (14 September 1957).
2 Bill Brugger, *China: Liberation and Transformation 1942–1962* (London: Croom Helm, 1981), 181.
3 Brugger, 239.
4 Brugger, 239.
5 Brugger, 239–240.
6 HKMS 158-1-283: 'HT Morgan (Commonwealth Office) to MacLehose (Foreign Office)' (23 May 1963), [2].
7 R.T. Naylor, *Hot Money and the Politics of Debt* (Montreal: MacGill-Queens University Press, 2004), 202.
8 Naylor, 202.
9 Naylor, 202.
10 Naylor, 202.
11 Brugger, 236.
12 Brugger, 236.
13 Brugger, 236.
14 HKMS 158-1-283 CO1030/1605 Telegram: 'EG Willan to Higham, Commonwealth Office' (27 June 1963), [2].
15 HKMS 158-1-283: Telegram: 'MacLehose (Foreign Office) to EG Willan (Chief Secretary)' (2 August 1963).
16 HKMS 158-1-283: 'MacLehose to EG Willan'.

72   1963

17 HKMS 158-1-283 CO1030/1605: Telegram: 'Sir R Black to Secretary of State for Commonwealth' (8 July 1963), [1].
18 CIA-RDP80-00809A000600340704-2: 'KMT Agents Continue Sabotage' (17 July 1950).
19 HKMS 158-1-283 CO 1030/1605: 'Extract LIC Report for May' (29 April 1963).
20 HKMS 158-1-283 CO1030/1605: Richard Hughes, 'Hong Kong Rounds up Formosa Spies' *Sunday Times* (9 June 1963), 4 ('Hughes' hereafter).
21 HKMS 158-1-283 CO1030/1605, Telegram 557 'KMT Guerrillas: Sir R Black to Secretary of State for Commonwealth' (8 July 1963), [1].
22 Hughes, 4.
23 Hughes, 4.
24 HKMS 158-1-283: 'Quarterly L.I.C Report' (20 July 1963).
25 HKMS 158-1-283: 'Quarterly L.I.C Report' (20 July 1963).
26 HKMS 158-1-283: 'Sir R Black (Governor) to Secretary of State for Commonwealth' (31 July 1963), [1].
27 HKMS 158-1-283: Reuters Report: 'Saboteurs have been working through Hong Kong in recent months – Hau Sang case' (30 July 1963), [1].
28 HKMS 158-1-283 (1030/1605): 'KN Coates (Immigration and Nationality) to MacLehose (Foreign Office)' (3 September 1963).
29 HKMS 158-1-283 CO1030/1605 Telegram: 'Sir R Black to Secretary of State for Commonwealth' (15 August 1963), [1].
30 See Explosive Substances Ordinance (Cap 206) s 4 & s 6.
31 Hughes, 4.
32 Hughes, 4.
33 HKMS 158-1-283 CO1030/1605: 'Mr Higham (Colonial Office) to Mr Pearce' (29 April 1963) [2].
34 HKMS 158-1-283: 'Quarterly L.I.C Report' (20 July 1963).
35 Steve Tsang, 'Strategy for Survival: The Cold War and Hong Kong's Policy Toward Kuomintang and Chinese Communist Activities in the 1950s' *Journal of Imperial and Commonwealth History* vol. 25, no. 2, 2008: 299.
36 Johannes Lombardo, 'A Mission of Espionage, Intelligence and Psychological Operations: The American Consulate 1949–1964' in Richard Aldrich, Gary Rawnsley and Ming Yen Rawnsley (eds), *The Clandestine Cold War in Asia* (New York: Frank Cass, 2000), 202.
37 Lombardo, 202.
38 HKMS 158-1-283 CO1030/1605: Telegram: 'Sir R Black to Secretary of State for the Colonies' (12 June 1963), [2].
39 HKMS 158-1-283 CO1030/1605: Telegram: 'Sir R Black', [2].
40 HKMS 158-1-283: 'HT Morgan (Commonwealth Office) to MacLehose (Foreign Office)' (23 May 1963), [2].
41 HKMS 158-1-283; CO 1030/1605: 'The Chief Secretary E.G. Edward Willan to Higham, Commonwealth Office' (27 June 1963).
42 HKMS 158-1-283: 'Extract LIC Report for May'.
43 CCP, China Handbook Editorial Committee, *History* (Peking: Foreign Languages Press, 1982), 185.
44 HKMS 158-3-1: 'Telegram 5: Secretary of State for the Commonwealth to Sir A Grantham' (20 October 1956).
45 e.g. CIA-RDP78-00915R001300230001-1: 'Communist Theory on Use of Violence and Guerrilla Warfare' (28 March 1961).

46 CIA-RDP82-00457R002900650006-7: 'Attitude of Kuomintang (KMT) in Thailand toward Communist Victory in China' (28 July 1949), 1.
47 CIA-RDP82-00457R008500400005-3: 'Chinese Communist Military Activities in Southern China 2. Chinese Communist Naval Activities' (1 September 1951), [2].
48 CIA-RDP89B00569R000800020002-3: 'Preliminary Evaluation of Mission 3241 Flown in 16 November 1963' (20 November 1963), [3].
49 CIA-RDP75B00380R000300080001-4, Frank Browning and Banning Garrett, 'The New Opium War' (5 January 1971) (unidentified magazine article cutting).
50 CIA-RDP75B00380R000300080001-4: 'New Opium War'.
51 CIA-RDP75-00149R000400360002-0, 'Warren Unna, "Burma Gets Military Aid Unannounced"' (1 June 1961), 13 ('Warren Unna' hereafter).
52 Warren Unna, 13.
53 Warren Unna, 13.
54 Warren Unna, 13.
55 HKMS 158-1-283: 'HT Morgan (Commonwealth Office) to MacLehose (Foreign Office)' (23 May 1963), [2].
56 CIA-RDP79-T00975A005400500001-6: 'Central Intelligence Bulletin' (28 December 1960), 2.
57 HKMS 158-1-283 (CO 1030/1605): 'Telegram No 466: HM Consul Peking to Foreign Office' (13 July 1963).
58 HKMS 158-1-283 (CO 1030/1605): 'MacLehose to EG Willan' (2 August 1963).
59 HKMS 158-1-283: 'EG Willan to CM MacLehose' (28 June 1963), [2].
60 HKMS 158-1-283: 'Rt Hon Philip Noel-Baker M.P. to Nigel Fisher M.P.' (22 May 1963), [1].
61 HKMS 158-1-283: 'Philip Noel-Baker'.
62 Ting-hong Wong, *Hegemonies Compared: State Formation and Chinese School Politics in Postwar Singapore and Hong Kong* (New York: Routledge, 2002), 15.
63 HKMS 158-3-1 440/01 'Telegram 3: Secretary of State for Commonwealth Alan Lennox-Boyd to Sir A. Grantham' (20 October 1956), [2].
64 HKRS 184-4-21: 'Telegram: A. Grantham', [14].
65 Carol Jones and John Vagg, *Criminal Justice in Hong Kong* (Oxford: Routledge, 2007), 101.
66 HKRS 169-2-119: 'Records Commander in Chief Hong Kong': 'Telegram: CIC Hong Kong to N.A. Chungking' (13 October 1945).
67 HKRS 169-2-119: 'Telegram: State Officer (Intelligence) Hong Kong to Chief of Staff' (11 October 1945), [1].
68 HKRS 169-2-119: 'Telegram: State Officer'.
69 HKRS 169-2-119: 'Telegram: NA Chungking to CIC Hong Kong' (6 October 1945), [1].
70 HKRS 169-2-119: 'Telegram: NA Chungking'.
71 HKRS 169-2-119: 'Following MacDougal for Wallinger' (undated).
72 HKRS184-4-21: (5/1162/48): 'Telegram: Government House Sir A. Grantham to A. Creech-Jones' (28 May 1948), [6].
73 HKRS184-4-21: 'Telegram: A. Grantham', [6].
74 HKRS184-4-21: 'Telegram: A. Grantham', [6].
75 HKRS 184-4-4 (6/761/48): 'Government House Hong Kong Sir A. Grantham to HBM Embassy Nanking' (24 June 1948).

76 HKRS 184-4-4-4 6/761/48: 'Telegram: A. Grantham'.
77 HKRS 184–4–21 (5/1162/48): 'Telegram: Government House Sir A. Grantham to A. Creech-Jones' (28 May 1948), [10].
78 W.P. Morgan, *Triad Societies in Hong Kong* (London, Routledge, 2000), 64.
79 Morgan, 64–65.
80 Morgan, 65.
81 HKMS 158-1-283: 'HT Morgan to M. MacLehose (Far Eastern Dept, Foreign Office)' (23 May 1963), [1].

4 Anatomies examined

Introduction

This book has detailed the political recognitions and resistances inside and outside of Hong Kong in the 1950s, progressed to analyse what causation claims of the riot of 1956 favourable to the KMT suggested about the anatomy of Hong Kong colonialism and given details explaining the British administration's rapprochement toward the Chinese communists in 1963.

Those seeking to negate histories of colonial-era violence tend to explain its consequences by following tributaries, not rivers. The old colonial powers arrived at their current-day humanist pacifism, and its appeals to collectivist internationalism, after benefiting from a long period of sustained violence against colonised people aimed at their subjugation. Lingering colonials offering long-suffering native others an opportunity to use technical knowledge to arrive at enlightened humanism could be forgivable if given over in the spirit of a short-cut. But it was not. It was a hoax implying an apprenticeship in material improvement was a big deal, although it was only ever offered when an unimpeachable advantage had already been gained. For the time being, Hong Kong has lived up to its colonial dream of becoming a thin-distributing democracy of hustlers protected from the orthodoxies of communism by cultivating an inward-looking gaze. But those days are surely as numbered as its technical advantage.

The champions of old colonial Hong Kong imagined it nestling into a provincial China based on a model of multi-national federalism. The communist credo of a unitary nation under a government that centralised power in a national capital made that impossible. The colonial fantasy of ushering Hong Kong, fortified in its capitalism, into a negotiated national polity, mistook the New China for the old. The concept of 'One Country, Two Systems' encourages belief in Hong Kong's special status. Rather, the British administration in Victoria and grandees of Whitehall abandoned their colony to the grip of communist influence, then recovered it, on an ad hoc basis, losing their grip a little more every time they wrenched their colony back.

Hong Kong's independence after 1945 turned on whether or not it felt to the British that the U.S. State Department, looking over its shoulder, graded them on their anti-communism. The gradual release to a negotiated 'special case' within China has been a British explanation tending to mask the reality of colonial Hong Kong jumping in and out of the national unity sought by the CCP. The reality of adept British accommodations with Chinese communism has been masked by a colonial anatomy claiming it was underpinned by political indifference, a wait-and-see policy or the romance of righteous stoicism.

Hong Kong nevertheless occupies an underrated place in the modern history of the Chinese nation. Tibet, Xinjiang and Taiwan remain locales in China where, as Duara framed it, 'nationhood continues to have different meanings among those who still have the means to express their difference'.[1] Much the same could be said of Hong Kong. This study has played a small part in describing the waxing and waning of colonial Hong Kong in a history of Chinese unitary government. It began with ignored communist squeaks of protest in 1956, the knee-jerk British appeasement of the communists in 1963 and, as other histories have shown, climaxed in decisive communist action to foment anti-capitalist trouble in 1967.

One could infer from this text that British southern China colonialism and Chinese communism were antithetical philosophies. Yet their eventual reconciliation over the policy to be applied to suicidal KMT agents running amok in Guangdong indicated a détente of sorts. Practical reasons prompted it. Hong Kong authorities needed breathing space from communist interference without it showing inside the colony itself. Hong Kong needed China to save it from recurring water shortages, and Whitehall needed a principled example of foreign policy independent of the Americans due to Albion's loss of colonial top dog status after the rout of Singapore.

Underneath the interplay of pragmatics and anatomical symbolism, two new policy realities slid in after 1956. Chinese communism was not absolutist on the foreign policy stage in the way the Russians typified it, and British colonialism was no longer advanced by diplomacy breathtakingly at odds with reality, as it had been in the old days when pointing out the contradiction of colonial anatomy risked a gunboat salvo and invasion of a port with foreign traders brandishing the treaty-given rights of most-favoured nation status. During the 1950s, neither China nor the United Kingdom had will enough to enact its anatomical self-image as foreign policy. This penultimate chapter overlays the philosophical schemas of colonialism and communism as anatomical ideologies. It also offers an assessment of the Kuomintang's political platform after 1949. The symbolic Sino-British détente of 1963 suggested that how each ideological system viewed an individual can be a profitable area to explore as a thread of historical inquiry. Let it be essayed that a diplomacy developed between Peking and Whitehall based on strategic recognition of convergence: issues that were sacrosanct to one that mattered nothing to the conceder, and vice versa. A concession on such a point cost the conceder nothing and created goodwill in the other. Pragmatic symbolism such as the Sino-British détente over KMT bomb throwers in 1963 required neither side to be driven out of town as a heretic to its creed. It could only ease the pressure. Episodes such the forced foreign exodus from Shanghai in the years leading up to 1949 and Hong Kong's eruption in 1967 formed unavoidable collision points for both political systems. This makes reconciliatory gestural politics either false liberality or a brief convergence of anatomy and an underlying legitimacy.

Much of this book has been about ideology and, particularly, how anatomy is projected as substance but in reality is a façade. In this penultimate chapter, I add another example testing the colonial anatomy from its compensation chronicles. The case of Chau Yuen Szi joins the Leung Tong case from Chapter 2 in witness to a presumptive legal category of low-level opportunists and hapless bystanders who absorbed more than a small share of liability for the riot of 1956. After characterising the British colonial anatomy, and that of the KMT, this chapter highlights the shortcomings of the CCP anatomy evident its inconsistent messaging to Chinese diaspora populations living outside the motherland.

The colonial anatomy

One could say that politically ambivalent southern Chinese businessmen were bound to be overrepresented in the compensation arrangements of Hong Kong because the colony had become a preferred refuge for so many of them after 1949. Yet an average local businessman expressing a political want was an import-export tout and anti-communist financier in equal parts. The KMT's central committee in Taipei held fast to a policy of conducting sabotage raids and assassination missions in southern China from 1950 to 1963, as well as occasional pipe bomb outrages against communist-owned property or symbolic targets in the colony.

The British administration in part blamed the 1956 riot on overly zealous KMT agents, but left their response there and did not conceive nationalist violence in terms of resistance to colonialism. By constructing inside the colony a matrix of 'good' KMT merchants and a 'naughty' militants, the colonial administration could promote the 'good' ones with commercial opportunity turning a blind eye to 'naughty' ones to be funded by local patrons and U.S. congressmen. The anatomy of colonial Hong Kong was comprised of a subdermal layer of ambivalence to Rightism under a heralded skin of indifference.

The anatomy of the British of Hong Kong and Whitehall was enmeshed with the fate of fellow opportunists. Opportunism could not be called an exclusively KMT passion. Communists were seasoned traders in post-war Hong Kong. The main tension between the colonial administration of Hong Kong and the U.S. State Department administrations of the 1950s was the so-called China Differential policy – an embargo introduced in December 1950 by the Americans that made it more difficult to trade with China than Russia. Perversely, it created a communist-driven trade in Hong Kong requiring fronts including Norwegian-registered ships, Brazilian buyers and a trading culture based, for the right price, on Hong Kong officialdom ignoring the provenance of anyone and anything, with some exceptions including munitions bound for the Korean peninsula via Hong Kong and Liaoning.

Despite the implication of British colonial authority with KMT and communist opportunism, the historical story of Hong Kong plays down the questions raised by violence and its role in the formation of the colonial anatomy. One of the key questions investigated in these pages has concerned the extent of British responsibility for supporting KMT riot violence and terrorism in southern China after the Chinese civil war. Those afflicted by willful blindness to the imperial contribution to violence in colonies, and its influence on modern affairs, hold a default position in today's historiographical debates. In his view that 'the endeavour to find "a general theory" of terrorism . . . is a futile and misguided exercise', Laqueur, for instance, joined a brigade dismissing the colonial past as a way understand post-colonial dilemmas including the reminiscences and snatches of irredentism or the successes of violent extremism and lingering totalitarianism.[2] Wilkinson cultivates this conceit as well: 'there is no adequate and generally accepted scientific theory of political violence or of political terrorism'.[3] Whether one considers the two days and two nights of unchecked KMT rioting in Hong Kong in 1956, or their violent cross-border resistance to communist forces in China from 1950 to 1963, neither can be easily designated as examples of finished business, or too complex to be characterised in influential terms. There can be no denying the importance of distant violence to set a pattern for current-day political interactions contemplating the political consequences of economic freedom or its potential role as a legacy and inspiration to modern separatist sentiments in Hong Kong or elsewhere in China, such as Taiwan. Nor can colonial indifference to assassination violence and cross-border outrages assist a nostalgic memory of its modus.

There are problems with Wilkinson's position denying a contemporary schema to historical violence, because the colonial moment has vanished. Although, like his peers, he acknowledged revolutionary terrorist violence was well-suited to wars of national liberation, and had sense enough to regard the word 'terrorist' as usually quite meaningless, he had no interest in challenging narrow causation readings for post-colonial power in a post-1945 world of Britain diminished by new powers, or ascribing modern day militarist reaction to sinews deep in colonial-era brutality.

Colonial states created conditions for a chain of grudges. When the grudges hold, if not presented in the West as violence that is spontaneous and mindless, or as a futile complaint against economic asymmetry, they are portrayed as hopeless separatism against the natural order of things. Ongoing geopolitical tensions caused by Hong Kong and Taiwan seem to find their deflections in every place except the colonial past, too. Western historians are driven to the likes of Laqueur and Wilkinson for comforts of Western liberal critique. When such commentators are put to a choice of supporting violent resistance or the economic asymmetry of post-colonialism, their preference for the latter could not be clearer. They have explained and maintained post-colonial anatomies for a living, and the historians cheer them on.

The old liberals will not see current conditions as toxic colonial history or principled rejection of democratic constitutionalism. This has spread to the country club agenda in the histories of the KMT Three. This trio prefers to tally the human cost of socialist revolution in China in order to conclude that its purgative cost too much. For them, it is beyond comprehension that China required no less than a social exorcism to get rid of Western influence to pursue its own path. They do not believe in clean breaks in history when they are at the expense of their colonial forebears, either. Under that lens, the history of what happened in China was more important in consequence for the West, than for China itself. Dikötter has argued that China was not a moribund state in the republican years nor in need of a revolutionary rebirth; the country was politically open, diplomatically successful in achieving territorial unity and a site of a cultural renaissance.[4] Dikötter and Bickers prefer to write about the sovereign rights achievement of the KMT government in the 1930s as if the West ever wanted a united China or had made resisting the Japanese aggression in Manchuria in 1931 a defining moment – which it didn't.

Any observer who denies that the communist victory in China was the choice of a deliberative, politically assimilated populace has a perverse grasp on the country's history. The Chinese Communist Party rejected the influence of foreigners in their country but grew ever-more diverse itself. Membership of the CCP in 1949 stood at 1.2 million and, by 1956, it had grown to 10.7 million members.[5] It was observed in one report that 'the gates of the party had been opened to a growing influx of opportunist and career-ist elements'.[6] Loh, putting troop strength of the CCP in the final years of the civil war at two million, declared that 'many . . . were defectors from the KMT'.[7] Such rude realities contradict the 'openness and democracy' argument of Dikötter in solicitude to the previous republican government[8] and the communism-free history of China favoured by the likes of Bickers.

By describing colonial and communist anatomies, my purpose has been to reveal dissonant tones. What people proclaim in their daily life can only be incidental in an archive. It is not often that a refrain of colonial shame is heard in an archive, and if it is, it is an overlooked morsel of evidence or thought not to disclose anything important throughout decades of mis-taken curation. The best one can do in an archive is to seek documents that resonate to a certain pitch. This is often a fruitless aim. The passage of time and inscrutable rules conspire so that nothing beyond the low hum-ming noise of the air conditioners can be detected. Yet during research for this project, I managed to hear a lamentable refrain that alerted me to the anatomy of colonialism: the abortive compensation cases of Mr Leung Tong (Mrs Ho Mo Ching) and Mrs Chau Yuen Szi.

The Chau case

In the British Far Eastern possessions after a riot, a well-established bureau-cratic practice dealt with dependents of those who had died. The colonial administration would ask all such dependents to supply it with a written application for compensation. Unless an application was received, the administration would not reveal where the body of the dead person was buried or interred. The practice stood as a convenient reminder of how colonialism worked, or put another way, the reality beneath the anatomy. Whether or not the loved one was granted access to their deceased relative's remains depended on making a finding of whether or not the individual was a rioter. Such was the inquiry in the case of Mrs Chau.

Mrs Chau Yuen Szi, aged 61 was native to Tung Kum (south of Wen-zhou on the mainland). She went through this process regarding her son who died on the junction of Kwong Wah and Tung Choi Streets, Kowloon on 11 October 1956 (Figure 4.1). She wrote to the Inspector of the Riot Compensation Advisory Board advising that she had been given a cemetery permit that she relinquished with her application for compensation, that it had been 'revealed that no compensation may be awarded'.[9] Mrs Chau asked if the cemetery permit could be returned to her as soon as possible 'so that there is a trace as to where the deceased has been buried'.[10] This meant that the mandated supply of an application for compensation was

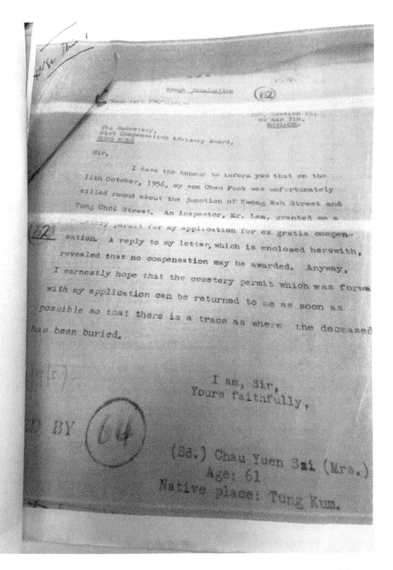

Figure 4.1 Mrs Chau's begging letter to the Colonial government of Hong Kong (1957)

interpreted as an attempt by a family member to displace a presumption of guilt of the dead person for participating in a riot.

An old-fashioned bit of blackmail, the colonial actions said: unless you cooperate in the process, you will never have a hope of seeing the resting place of your deceased. What seems most inconsistent with British anatomical projections of presumptive justice was that the cemetery permit was returned with the application, leaving a presumption that cooperative relatives who were deemed unworthy of being compensated would not gain access to the remains of their relative, at least not without a special subsequent request. People who had no direct hand in the riot were quickly reduced to begging for the remains of those who presumably did.

Despite their professed sympathies for Chinese people in Hong Kong, the communists in the colony would have characterised British colonial behaviour such as the treatment of Mrs Chau as quite apt for her mothering a delinquent Rightist thug. This would sit easily with their broader theme that the colonial government had responsibilities to deserving Chinese workers who were disappointed by low or no compensation and not having their unprovoked stab wounds taken seriously. One civil servant remarked that it was regularly said in colonial government circles that the People's Republic would get upset 'if services in Hong Kong were too markedly in advance of those in China' and conceded that such an argument had 'an element of immorality'.[11] There was no objection by communist Chinese in 1956–1957 to the working people of Hong Kong receiving better treatment than they did. They had a strong idea that the British followed a rigged 'laissez-faire' model in the compensation arrangements of the colony, but such knowledge did not translate to influence within it because it was not the right time to make a decisive example of colonial rule.

Mrs Chau's case showed how the agents of colonialism presumed the worst of its 'native' subjects and cared nothing about being cast as an enemy in their eyes. The Chinese have a proverb that 'it is easier to go up a mountain and catch a tiger than it is to open one's mouth and ask for help'. This underscores an element of personal pride felt by many Chinese people when seeking assistance, but in the example of Mrs Chau, her humiliation of having a son viewed as having an indeterminate or guilty role in the riot could only have been added to by having to beg a foreign country's authorities to tell her where his body lay.

The tendency to add insult to injury was not coded in the DNA of colonialism alone; it crossed into post-colonial descriptions of fairness, justice, etc. Nevertheless, in the case of Mrs Chau and the earlier example of Mr Leung Tong, and his widow Mrs Ho Mo Ching, the British compensation authorities put store in compensation recipients being able to give evidence that their dead family member was not, say, sprayed by colonial Greener gun pellets while they were hoisting sacks of rice out of an unguarded warehouse. A family member had to be fatally defending their own property to prove themselves on the right side of history. Timid use of a compassionate compensation category by the colonial government for lightly evidenced claims made it clear how its anatomy of civilian compensation and the reality of it fully supporting KMT factory rebuilds were worlds apart.

Hong Kong history has in large part been written by whites for white memory. Yet the reason why history remains seldom taught in Hong Kong is not that it is business-obsessed, too factional, or dominated by a master-race narrative. Rather, the resonances sought by its people in history have not come to the fore, have not pierced the background hum of the archive. The atonalities that history sweeps aside might prove melodic and affirming to those yet to hear their songs. The prospects of developing good Hong Kong history are much like those of any post-colonial history waiting in the wings. Without historians, local and imported alike, vitally concerned to write from a disinterested utilitarian narrative, reputable Hong Kong history will remain an exception rather than a rule.

The midst of divide-and-rule colonialism was no testing ground for universal rights and, thus, anatomical evolution was impossible. By offering a legalistic anatomy of the who, when and where of the riot of 1956, the colonial government's compensation regime constituted a late colonial grope at rule-bound impartiality. It failed a simple test of self-awareness. It made no attempt to hide its bias toward the right kind of KMT commercial and underworld representatives, or consider that its hostility to the claims of the communists had a slow-burning consequence.

By refraining from an egalitarian compensation program, yet sharing the blame for riot violence around to include the communists, the British anatomy risked not being able to break through to its public. It prevented it from taking cover behind an *audi alteram* argument, too. When cooperation with the Chinese communists finally occurred, it was out of British colonial desperation, and put in terms of expediency, rather than principle, indicating that the cherished anatomy of equanimity died hard.

The communist anatomy

As one communist observed, since 1925, one of the articles of faith for an imperialist in China was that 'all unequal treaties should remain in force because China is still in a state of "internal disorder" '.[12] This was answered easily by its critics who maintained that the pathology of imperialism relied on making extraterritoriality a weasel-word for national enfeeblement caused by enforced opium addiction and selectively leaving jurisdiction to separatist warlordism.

The awful idea of the country being unfit for anything but colonialism still held significance for Hong Kong in 1956. By then, of course, the unequal treaty days were swept away as an explanation for colonialism by the ascendance of the communists on the mainland in 1949. Nevertheless, there had been a century-old tradition of the foreign powers presiding over their colonial enclaves, and preserving commercial calm with gunboats and garrisons, if need be. The role of colonialism in CCP ideology is an important consideration.

A riot in any British colonial redoubt embarrassed its authorities because law and order assumed a much larger importance when a government had no popular legitimacy. A government voted in or resulting from a popular revolution could say that the discontent expressed in a riot came from a minority. The communist line on this was very clear in their published comments in the newspapers of 1956 and 1957: if the British in Hong Kong were to run the place as a fiefdom of gangsters and foreigners, at least they could get the policing right so people could go about their daily lives without running a gauntlet of cleavers and boning knives.

Considering the Mao-induced chaos in southern China and elsewhere in the country in the postcode purges of 1950–1951, the appeal of local communists to law and order as an example of how things were done in the motherland constituted a large clue to the bankruptcy of the communist anatomy. In the early 1950s, the communist anatomy stressing high sounding ideals for the progress of the nation screened the murderous reality of anti-Rightist purges, strategic accommodations with capitalist Hong Kong and surprising existential doubts when countering KMT misinformation campaigns over the war in Korea.

The colonial secretary refused to meet complaining communist delegations after the 1956 riot, and that was in no small part due to their constant reiteration that the colonial government lacked legitimacy. They usually left a letter for him before returning to their welfare centres, looms and paddy fields in a huff. This brings us to the question of the communist anatomy and what it disguised. It centred on 'the people' – who they were and how the CCP asserted its representation of their interests. I write not of the bourgeois economism of the party these days, or not directly at least, but rather of historical precedents of Leftism in China that united in reaction to colonialism, and were claimed by the CCP. The communist anatomy had to be more than a critique blaming many of China's woes on colonialism; it needed to be a people's movement standing for something more than opposition to foreigners.

The communist Chinese reading of the events of 1860 was that the imperial powers ultimately sided with a traduced Manchu government against the boorish Taiping army which had nevertheless 'always preserved the basic qualities that derive from a revolutionary peasant war'.[13] This enabled the Manchus to continue in their 'conservatism, depravity, corruption and ineptitude' while making a claim to side with 'decent Chinese' and allowing the foreigners to continue enjoying their benefits under the unequal Treaty of Tientsin and the Convention of Peking.[14]

In a similar vein to the communist deployment of the Taiping tradition, because Sun Yat-sen in 1922–1924 announced a program of a Soviet alliance, cooperation with the CCP and progressing the conditions of the peasants and the proletariat, historians of the CCP have claimed him as a proto-communist, albeit one with fluctuating mass appeal who rather too much lurked about the secret societies stitching up shady constituencies. Both the Taiping and Sun Yat-sen examples have situated the CCP as inheritors of the people's wishes and awaiting its historical moment to lead. It comes through strongly in their repetitious Hong Kong propaganda after 1956. Thus, historicist fatalism and anti-revisionism are key parts of the CCP anatomy, even though its underlying reality could be a confused mix of pro-colonial and anti-colonial, benevolent-sounding to the diaspora Chinese and, as we shall note soon, insincere toward them as well. What else lay beneath the communist anatomy in a colony such as Hong Kong?

Communist propaganda implored the colonial government of Hong Kong 'to take concrete steps to protect lives and property of workers and residents and to prevent any recurrence of riots' and expressed 'dissatisfaction over the failure of the Government to check the riots in time and the unreasonable compensation awarded'.[15] This implied that a communist-controlled Hong Kong would have protected its people by foreseeing the riots before they occurred and locked down Kowloon until all troublemakers were rounded up. Their propaganda always situated themselves as having Janus-like powers of perception. Yet this improbability suggests them holding a conception of history as it was jointly agreed rather than one that valued what happened. The quality of selective falseness they decry in colonial history as driving them to seek the authenticity of 'the people' has become a two-edged sword. One cannot claim 'the people' then play down the occasions when you fail them. This was because no margin of error had been given in the anatomy of the CCP to colonialism, except when colonialism was obviously useful.

Mixed messages

Once the CCP came to power in mainland China in 1949, its external affairs policy faced a mighty question: did party propaganda extend an olive wreath to diaspora Chinese populations throughout East and South East Asia, or did its paternalism express itself as a highly conditional love for those Chinese who remained outside the motherland after end of the civil war? The result in the case of the CCP's attitude to the ex-KMT military personnel in Hong Kong in November 1950 can be seen in Figure 4.2. It expresses an irksome triumphalism that assures the refugees that 'your government will be generous to you all', although they are deemed 'traitors to your own country' who needed to reflect on 'the crimes you have committed' and 'repent'.[16]

Such a sour offer of years in re-education in order to begin again at the lowest rung of Chinese society should be compared with an upbeat article addressed to diaspora Chinese in the *Ta Kung Pao* newspaper, Shanghai edition, earlier in the year in January 1950. It announced that the P.R. China had established diplomatic recognition with several Asian countries and that, as a result, 'the more than ten million Overseas Chinese shall and must not be subjected to further abuse'.[17] The article referred to the new Chinese Constitution requiring the People's Government to 'do its utmost to protect the legitimate rights of Chinese residing abroad' and that the Chinese of Thailand, Indo-China and Malaya were being 'persecuted' and that there existed an 'imperialist plot for both direct and indirect attack against the Chinese people'.[18]

After 1956, the CCP frequently – if unsuccessfully – tried to speak to the colonial government of Hong Kong on behalf of its Chinese residents. This was a rhetorical device claiming responsibility for the same people who, six years earlier, when housed in a refugee camp at Rennie's Mill were, according to the CCP, following 'illusory dreams' and needed to 'wake up' and return to China to face the consequences of fleeing.[19] One could draw a communist conclusion that, in the early 1950s, those Chinese fleeing China to Hong Kong were in a special category of diaspora Chinese needing communist discipline. As the years rolled by, such people remained exiled in their cross-border residences. They never sought the forgiveness of Mother China, nor warmed to it when the CCP sought to speak for them when British law and order broke down leaving them injured or killed. Yet, in 1950, when both statements were made, their inconsistency raised a question of which New China had come into being: a generous and protective republic of ideals, or a creepy, punitive one settling the score?

There were problems with the CCP anatomy after the 1956 riot, too. The CCP line in 1957 ordained that affiliated trade unionists not fill in 'Item 9, Form A' of the compensation documents requesting details of all sources of previous compensation. To keep the financial links between the mainland and Hong Kong communists secret, the constituent members of Hong Kong trade unions were impoverished by the very bodies who claimed to be there in support of them. Unemployment relief, rebuilding farmers' mat sheds, replacing irrigation equipment, giving keys to emergency housing, food

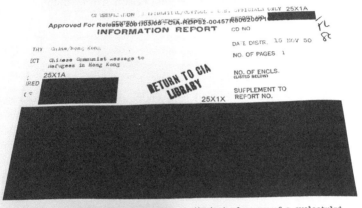

CLASSIFICATION CONFIDENTIAL/CONTROL - U.S. OFFICIALS ONLY 25X1A

Approved For Release 2000/05/08 : CIA-RDP82-00457R006200...

INFORMATION REPORT   CD NO

TRY   China/Hong Kong   DATE DISTR. 15 NOV 50

CT   Chinese Communist Message to   NO. OF PAGES 1
     Refugees in Hong Kong

25X1A   NO. OF ENCLS.
                                          (LISTED BELOW)
IRED

(SUPPLEMENT TO
                                   25X1X REPORT NO.

The following message was hand-written on the back of a copy of a cyclostyled
greeting which FANG Shih-ts'un (方通存), superintendent of the Hong Kong
refugee camp at Rennie's Mill, had distributed to the inmates of the camp on
the occasion of the Mid-Autumn Festival,

"Warning to the inmates of the refugee camp:
 You stateless and pitiful creatures!
 Yours is not the broad and bright path, for you are slaves of the
 imperialists and tools of the American brigands.
 You are enemies of your own people and traitors to your own country!
 Think again about the crimes you have committed.
 Turn your thoughts to your home country, repent and save your own people!
 Do not be duped by illusory dreams.
 Our government will be generous to you all.
 All you want to do is to go to Taiwan, and for this you exert every effort.
 Yet what happens? how many of you have actually got to Taiwan?
 Let me tell you - the People's Liberation Army will attack and liberate
 Formosa.
 Hong Kong is no paradise, for Hong Kong is also one of our objectives.
 Where, then, will you go? The British imperialists will not always be able
 to protect you.
 If you delay, it may be too late.
 Wake up! Stir yourselves, join the People's Government.

     Signed: WANG Chiu (王九)

Figure 4.2 Description of a Chinese communist note to ex-KMT soldiers in
   Hong Kong (1950)

security drives, etc. – in short, all of the things that unions could do for their membership – were put in jeopardy. This was just so that the local communist leadership could make a point that the British administration was stingy and did not care for Hong Kong's Chinese people. Of course, the colonial government did not really care, but the communists provoked it into dismissing them without them having filed a statement of claim. The communist refusal to help the police with their inquiries had a rather tangy odour, too, no matter how fetid the reek of the colonial police force and Special Branch.

Communism and rumours

After the Chinese civil war had officially ended, impotent gangster anger prevailed in the ranks of the KMT. Yet so, too, did a power to confuse the population of China. A tendency to nihilistic destruction had underlain the KMT's anatomy all along, and although it had been disguised during wartime, it was highlighted by its final failure to stave off the communists. Mao's anti-counter-revolution campaign commencing in October 1950 took no time in provoking a welter of misinformation, reactive espionage and armed revolts from the remaining KMT diehards.

In late October of 1950, a communist newspaper in Dairen (Dalian these days) reported an upsurge in counter-revolutionary rumours and activities throughout China to be remedied by holding mass meetings where apprehended rumourmongers were made to 'confess their evil doings'.[20] Information campaigns were launched to seek out enemy agents and 'stamp out false rumours'.[21] Most troubling to the communists were the rumours circulating about their bellicose and unnecessary prosecution of the Korean War. One beleaguered report conceded that, 'people who keep up with current events do not believe these false counterrevolutionary rumours, but there are many others who do'.[22]

A mass anti-rumour movement comprised of the 'study-the-current-events propaganda' was enacted by the communists 'to stop the enemy paralysing us'.[23] A meeting was held by the Public Security Bureau at the T'ieh-hsi Machinery Factory No. 1, where a worker helpfully proclaimed: 'we must be a hundred times more cautious and not believe false rumours. We must strive to increase production so that we can be able to stop the aggressive war started by the U.S. imperialists'.[24] By trying to prevent a dialectic of KMT and communist versions of events through enforcing intellectual isolationism on the KMT, the communists assembled a version of history all their own. Yet the result of this victory was a murderous mathematical reprisal conducted by the CCP that was resisted, in turn, by KMT propaganda about the wastefulness of the Korean War and by launching guerrilla resistance actions in southern China.

The divergent versions of southern China history remain unreconciled meaning that little progress has been made since the old communist history of Rightist rumour-mongering, which itself discloses a measurable tendency to paranoia and neurosis. Admirers of the KMT Three persist with a history that communists buried landlords alive and KMT heroes liberated granaries for villagers. Not only does the today's CCP rarely dignify them with debate, the early 1950s remains a seldom-recalled period of China's story, owing to the fact the CCP were such bad winners.

The CCP played a disingenuous game for hearts and minds in Hong Kong in 1951. Much of it was driven by its sensitivity to anti-communist Korean War propaganda produced in the colony in that year. In one example, the party stepped up arrests and executions of men who had defected to them from the KMT and returned to Canton after a period of service in Hong Kong.[25] Those executed, including Lo Yao-chang and Li Yueh-ting, had formerly been part of the KMT's Bureau of Information and Statistics. They had failed to induce newspaper men in Hong Kong to return to Canton because, in 1950, several returnee journalists had been executed by the communists when they delivered themselves in good faith to Canton.[26] An element of the assassination culture and strong part of the futile mission of inducing wary potential returnees were examples of ex-KMT communist operatives in Hong Kong needing to prove themselves to their new paymasters. The purge mentality of the CCP in southern China was the reality behind the anatomy of playing nicely with capitalists in Hong Kong by disappearing their enemies to quiet rendition sites in the countryside of China.

Learning from the peasants

Not all histories of China written by Westerners have accentuated communist failures or the saving graces of the KMT. Nor is reliance on communist histories authored by approved committees entirely necessary for those seeking a different way of thinking about this particular contested past. French historians Jean Chesneaux and Lucian Bianco revealed much about the communist intellectual tradition in China. They did so in a manner that did not simply describe it as a peasant revolution that fell like an enormous vermilion blanket from the sky in 1949 to stifle everything beneath it. The rationalisations of Chinese communism shift, gain momentum and are discarded in favour of new ideas. The relationship of rationale to behaviour is the measure of any ideology. However, whether communist anatomy enlivened life as it is lived would seem a particularly sensitive issue for it. Updating language can be explained as inevitable in a pursuit of modernity, but abandoning origins carries a risk that its purpose has been lost.

For Chesneaux, there were two sides to Chinese communism: (1) that of Liu Shao-ch'i emphasising measured economic progress under Five Year Plans, dualism of state and party, and pursuing the latest technology in heavy industry and (2) that of Mao highlighting peasant originalism, the input of the masses in public policy, and agriculture at the base of the economy.[27] Thus, there was a tension between Soviet-style industrial managerialism and Chinese traditionalism favouring agrarian philosophical authenticity over technique. It explains much about how Chinese communist ideology became a synthesis of technology in service of equality.

Bianco's contribution was to recognise the May 4th intellectual movement of 1919 as the basis of Marxism in China, at first co-opting its iconoclasm, and later extinguishing its liberalism with doctrinal discipline imagined to be revolutionary radicalism.[28] Supporters of the May 4th movement took anti-colonialism as its foundational idea, but adopted Western reason to make attacks on Confucian tradition in its institutional heartlands. They took every opportunity to highlight their democratic credentials and pro-science cosmopolitanism.

As the events of 1966–1969 demonstrated, the anti-restoration militancy of the Cultural Revolution in denouncing skill and experience meant that the ardour inspired by the May 4th movement's curse on tradition, for a short period of time, replaced economic planning and industrialisation as the CCP's anatomical projection. The anti-imperialism that inspired the May 4th movement was strong among the Red Guards, too; they renamed Hong Kong the 'Kick Out the Imperialists City', leading to a backflip by colonial authorities by ultimately allowing mail so addressed to pass into the colony.

How communist rule these days relates itself to earthy proverb entrenched in cultural currency, on one hand, and a selective appeal to New China modernity, on the other hand, seems like a new balance. But it is not. Its anatomical appeal lays in denying its tautology and inconsistency in history to make its reductions in favour of nation or individual appear to work with pragmatic ease. This ungainly quality on a close examination always formed part of Chinese communism in Bianco's view. 'How else can we imagine the triumph of the oppressed?'[29] he asked.

The colonial worry about the communists of Hong Kong, be they the long-faced ones with assassination on their minds, designated capitalists trading for the war in Korea, trade unionists or social workers dealing with unemployment and housing issues, was that they seldom had any peer in their knowledge of what was going on in Hong Kong. The British colonials, of course, could see how this informational advantage meant that their political positions were effortlessly gathered up and contorted in the communist narrative because this was exactly *their* modus toward the communists.

When both sides exaggerated their own position yet called it moderate, little common ground might be supposed. That is to say, the anatomising project had the same techniques, regardless of which side did it. Self-awareness was never a goal reached by an anatomiser, and could not result from critique from without. The mutual lack of self-awareness of communists and colonialists made a dialectical exchange between the two possible. It was because both were deaf that they could read each other's lips and respond to each other.

The communists could never be wrong about history if they all identified the same problems, reiterated them to their imperial foes without ceasing, and predicted trouble if they were not attended to promptly. In 1956–1957, the archival record was punctuated by three recurring communist claims:

1   '[T]he Hong Kong government should avoid not its responsibility in connection with the occurrence and consequence of the riots'.[30]
2   '[M]ore severe punishment should be meted out to those murders apprehended and Government should round up those culprits still at large so as to prevent future riots and uproot bad elements once for all'.[31]
3   The Government 'should shoulder the responsibility of making fair and reasonable compensation to those who suffered'.[32]

The colonial government's response to this, at least among its own members, was that they were 'well-nigh worn out demands'.[33] Each demand was a perfect statement explaining communist dissatisfaction with the colonial government response in 1956–1957. The demands also sketched out an anatomy for an unobtainable socialist state: big and protective, measured toward all and invested in a reckoning here on earth, justifying control by referring to harmony.

The CCP had legitimate grievances about what happened in Hong Kong in 1956. Communist members of Kowloon trade unions reported that many of them had been attacked and injured by rioters.[34] Some had been robbed of personal possessions and had to suffer hunger because they could not go to work. Another member reported payment of a paltry HK$288 as compensation for losses – an amount that did not keep the member in food while he recuperated.[35] These indignities were made worse for many local communists by the fact that Yeung Tat Yang, a KMT gangster and 'one of the most notorious culprits in the riots last year', continued to operate with a free hand in Tsuen Wan and, over in the cotton mills, a KMT fundraising drive was occurring to hold a meeting to mark the one year anniversary of the riot.[36] The KMT wanted to celebrate what it had done. Quite a remarkable feat, one could think, for a party that some allege had no responsibility for the riot.

In summary, the communist reality in Hong Kong was riven between being pro-colonial and anti-colonial, pro-Chinese diaspora and anti-Chinese diaspora, as well as pro- and anti-capitalist. It robbed credibility from the communist anatomy because it valued projecting revolutionary invincibility over policy consistency. Enforcing peasant wisdom looked especially like anti-modernity in Hong Kong, too.

The KMT anatomy

The KMT's southern China violence after 1949 was nihilistic, spontaneous and without hope of securing a national polity. But it was not a nullity. Its continuation underlined the fragility of the British administration's rationale for its continuing colonialism in Hong Kong. Colonial entrapment in pulses of obliged reward toward the KMT slowed the United Kingdom's post-colonial transition in East Asia and its development of a constructive relationship with communist China.

When in national government, the democratic republican anatomy of the Kuomintang could easily be given counterpoint by its inability to stop party members using air force planes to smuggle goods at an obscene premium to starving people, its hyperinflation-causing economic policies and violent purges of progressive elements in its own ranks. A major problem of the KMT after its final failures of 1949 lay in the inability of its intelligentsia to win over liberals outside China for the struggle to continue. Their redrawing of the KMT anatomy in response to the civil war failure and the gradual American funding retraction was a fascinating exercise, but was too little, too late, and led by unrepentant hierarchs in a sanctuary.

A group of dissident exiles in 1950s Hong Kong ran newspapers, schools, magazines and studious periodicals. Among them were middle- and upper-ranking elements of the old KMT regime, including vice-ministers, intellectual faction chiefs, a former secretary-general of the Legislative Yuan and former Yuan members. Hsuan T'ieh-wu was sent by the KMT Central Committee to Hong Kong in 1950 to coordinate the group in galvanising local anti-communist political voices.[37] It was reported in one CIA briefing that:

> The group is having very little success drawing to it anti-communist independent political elements. The presence in the group of P'eng Chao-hseng, Chang Kuo-t'ao and other who are well known as

members of the hardcore Kuomintang and the CC Clique has caused real liberals to shy away from any relationship with it.[38]

It cannot be surprising that the exiled KMT's anatomy sustained a fighting spirit after the war or that the party's Hong Kong group's program was designed 'to indicate to the world, and especially the United States, that the Kuomintang has support on the mainland of China and among Chinese intellectuals abroad'.[39] However, after 1949, its remnants in Hong Kong were seen as immoderate anti-communists who had survived precisely by being anti-intellectuals who had protected themselves by stockpiling for their American exodus and pointing a finger at suspected communist infiltrators of the party in the dying days of the civil war. The ideology and outlook of the communist Chinese did not have to be accepted. But the fact it won the civil war, and exercised the prerogatives of sovereignty that the KMT had enjoyed, were unavoidable realities.

Perhaps the most senior of the exiled KMT members in Hong Kong, T'ung Kuan-hsien, former president of the Legislative Yuan, declined to meet Hsuan and preferred to lead a quiet life. T'ung had been a follower of Li Tsung-jen. He had been a warlord, a militarist and a successful KMT general in northern China. An arch-supporter of the KMT, and avowedly anti-intellectual, he finally became a defector back to communist Peking in 1978 during an amnesty offered to those who wanted to return to the motherland.[40] A rare quality of T'ung's, at the very least, was that he knew when he had become too chequered by his experiences to play an upright role in contemporary politics. There was a fine line. On one hand, there was only so many times a line in political advocacy could be changed without credibility abandoning an individual; and on the other hand, after a seismic event like the loss of 1949, there existed a risk in maintaining consistency, i.e. not accepting defeat appeared to others like madness.

It would have been nihilist madness had the KMT old guard remnants of Hong Kong regrouped, rearmed then crossed the Hong Kong border *en masse* into the murder-by-postcode abyss of China 1950–1951. It was sardonic and self-preserving anti-communism that most remnant KMT types opted for, even if it failed the test of vehemence needed to defeat communism. The old guard was gradually absorbed into the body politic of Hong Kong, making their descendants conservative and anti-mainland Chinese in orientation, as if following a racial belief. In this process, the often ambiguous politics of their grandparents have been forgotten.

The old guard elites of the KMT had played hopscotch around the personalities of communism *par excellence*, making intrigue a way of life for much of the upper-middle class. An example in the Hong Kong group had been Chang K'uo-tao, who, in 1950, became a member of the KMT

Central Executive Committee based in the colony; he had once been asso-ciated with the communist Kiangsi provisional government.[41] KMT opera-tives posed as fellow communists to suspected communists, and as die-hard KMT members to suspicious members of the KMT. This became common among millions of people, making individual survival the foremost ideol-ogy of the KMT in the late 1940s rather than promoting a credible repub-lican vision.

The rescue of Shum Wai Yu

It was suggested earlier in this book that the colonial administration of Hong Kong cared less about a KMT partner's activities in mainland China than their track record in the colony. Shum Wai Yau exemplified the kind of KMT member that British colonialism loved and the anatomy of self-constrained free speech that it sought to promote. He also stands in com-parison to the estranged KMT factions who acted toward the British as they should: as representatives of a foreign government. He was an amoral operator who constantly stepped in and out of all bounds, except – it would appear – those of British favouritism because of his ostensibly supportive position during the Japanese Occupation of the colony. A character such as Shum could only exist because of the fragmented KMT anatomy. The KMT's inability to neutralise his type suggested that gaps of refuge for dissonant voices in colonialism made it all the more difficult to mount a credible anatomy.

Shum Wai Yu was editor of the *Overseas Chinese News* (*Wa Kiu Yat Po*). The newspaper had 'on the whole' been considered by the colonial admin-istration to have performed 'useful services' during the Japanese Occupa-tion.[42] The British colonial authorities rated Shum highly because he edited 'the only vernacular press to expound government policy'.[43] Indeed, the *Overseas Chinese News* survived from 1925 to 1995 as a Chinese daily news-paper affiliated with the *South China Morning Post*. The Chinese paper had its start in 1925 as an organ of record tasked with putting out government information about the riots during the Chinese boycott of Hong Kong to maintain the loyalty of Chinese workers in the port of Hong Kong. The *Overseas Chinese News* held the largest circulation of a Chinese daily and was counted among the wealthiest in Hong Kong. It continued through-out the Japanese Occupation alongside two other Chinese dailies by pub-lishing news 'between the lines'.[44]

Shum no doubt collaborated with the Japanese administration out of necessity. Authorities decided not to prosecute him after the war, because the likes of Robert Kotewall, Li Tze Fong, M.K. Lo and other leading Chinese also had 'hands not entirely clear'.[45] On the British account, the

KMT Political Studies Clique wanted to acquire the *Overseas Chinese News* on account of its wealth – not necessarily as an outlet for its propaganda, because it owned all other Chinese language daily newspapers in Hong Kong. That the KMT could not secure the deportation of a traitor or snatch away his control of a newspaper boded poorly for its claim of being part of the national government of China; it also looked immoderate and censorious in pursuing Shum.

In 1945, Shum was threatened with assassination by the CC Clique of the KMT and publication of his name on the Chinese 'Traitors List'.[46] Why this was thought to be the case was unclear. He moved in the circles of the conservative, anti-Japanese CC Clique, but had alienated himself from government cliques by appearing too clubby with the British, and had enjoyed a travel pass to Canton during the Japanese Occupation of Hong Kong. In fairness to Shum, it had been virtually impossible not to collaborate with the Japanese and stay alive throughout their occupation of Hong Kong. He requested assurance from the colonial government that it would not permit his extradition to Canton. To this, it replied that his extradition would only be allowed if he had committed some criminal offence in China.

In 1948, the Nationalist government applied successfully for the Hong Kong government to surrender General SK Yee under the Chinese Collaborators (Surrender) Ordinance, 1947. At this, Shum took fright. It led to him to sell his major interests in the *Overseas Chinese News*. He subsequently took British nationality to avoid extradition. The KMT could not let go of a nationalist anatomy based on being anti-Japanese, even when its increasingly fragmented government faced only the communist Chinese threat.

In a footnote to his case, a colonial file noted that Shum's subsequent efforts 'to shake off local KMT control' of his newspaper had been successful; even a ban on its circulation in Canton had been rescinded.[47] Shum presents a strong example of a KMT adherent who worked within the British colonial system and who withstood standover tactics with British help. That his fortunes were restored in Canton as well could only mean that he had been resurrected in elite KMT official circles representing Mo Hing Cheung in Hong Kong, or more likely, that Shum's position had been part of a thuggish ultimatum of the British administration to the local Nationalist elite. Shum was a useful example of how the British created a protected species among certain KMT members in Hong Kong. He was also a worthy example of how only a moderate loyalty to the British was needed in order to admit a Chinese subject to their protected status. That such a person was aware of the British deltas in the commercial tributaries of the colony, or did not always proceed with a surplus of rectitude or maintain unhelpful indifference, was usually quite enough to be named as a trustee in the British colonial camp.

Shum was a KMT factional loyalist who played within British law and order rules to receive commercial and political protection. In this sense, the British colonial government was a protection racket every bit as much as the KMT Political Studies Clique in Canton. The Shum case also suggested that a single case could describe a colonial fault line that threatened the British enterprise in Hong Kong to its foundations. In the case of Shum, there had been an article offensive to the colonial administration about the Shum affair in 1946, so its response had been to shut down the local Chinese paper owned by a rival faction of the KMT and cancel the Governor's impending visit to Canton.[48]

In a bureaucratic side comment in Shum's file, it was recorded: 'the article if unchallenged would suggest that the British sovereignty in Hong Kong might be ignored with impunity'.[49] By making Shum their man in 1948, the British administration of Hong Kong sent a similar message that obliging KMT members were welcome in Hong Kong. The colonial administration did not affect the KMT anatomy comprised of positions on democratic rights and China's territorial integrity, but by seeking out Shum for protection burnished its own liberal anatomy of permitting useful colonial partisans to stay and communists to have meetings.

Shum's case showed that the KMT's political perspective was honest and humanist in at least one respect: political relationships were treated like dance partners careering from one to another in an uncertain fate. Among the KMT, there was no communist-style disappointed loyalty ritualised and curtailed in a struggle session, or strategic accommodation in strictly controlled circumstances, as if there was a destiny higher than life. Not even the KMT's pragmatism and belief in opportunity, however, made redemption possible for those who had trucked with the Japanese fascists. By the late 1940s, the nationalist anatomy of the KMT had fallen into pursuing old grudges on outdated criteria. By the early 1950s, the expatriate KMT elements of Hong Kong had worn their anatomy so thin that Western sympathisers were becoming harder to find than before.

On occasion, the KMT's opportunism could stand out in good ways to promote progressive causes – including its modernist atheism and anti-monarchism, its edicts on maintaining personal health and its prosecutorial passion in the civil law tradition. It had upright spirits who cheered and hooped as legislation, science and reason dismantled feudalism's power structures, based as they were on an age-old fusion of untutored desire and military can-do. Nevertheless, its Godfather politics was not democracy, its endless corruption embarrassments were not transparency and its attempts at reform amounted to little more than investor confidence initiatives.

These were the realities its anatomy could not cover over. It was a coalition-ist anatomy that was not strong enough to see banished the antediluvian forces that sullied it.

The KMT's anatomy took inspiration from its high minds but did not promote them into leadership, except for a handful of American-trained economists when it was too late. It claimed to be the only democratic option in China capable of national government, undergoing genuine reform, the party of enlightenment under the fatherly watch of Sun Yat-sen, etc. Most historical commentators focus on its political disorganisation and corruption. They ridicule the fake reforms of militarist bagmen waving the pennant of democracy in exchange for hard currency so recklessly as to cause even the French franc to depreciate in China. Such perspectives unfairly consider nothing else than the corruption and factionalism of the KMT, making it unworthy of foreign support. It is not a great unfairness.

Conclusion

The anatomy of colonialism was revealed by the Chau case. The British colonial regime treated Mrs Chau as a presumed enemy because her son could not be cleared of doing something illegal during the riot. Yet there was no formal accusation by the riot compensation authority that he was a looter or murderer. Both the fruitless process of her pleading and the indif-ference of authorities tallies closely with the reality that compensation for individual civilians was pitifully low and scarce. Compounding the insult of colonial authority to Mrs Chau was the fact that she was still requesting its advice on the resting place of her son on 9 September 1957 – nearly a year after the riot. As such, this was an unremarkable example of an everyday distress caused by colonialism. At its kernel stood a government aloof from any accountability sought by an ordinary person caught in its shadow. This was the true nature of late colonialism beneath its anatomy of due process and compensation broadcast on a principled basis.

The two propaganda statements of 1950 were a disastrous mess for any CCP operative seeking to project a unified anatomy for Chinese commu-nism in Hong Kong. The disunity of the anatomy hinted strongly at an underlying reality. The CCP was still raw from the civil war and remained in purge mode against the KMT, but presumed leadership of cherry-picked overseas Chinese populations while soaking up the capitalist calm of Hong Kong. It would have been easier to forge an anatomy from an entirely vengeful position than wallpapering over such a conflicted state of affairs by explaining it as different messages for different constituencies.

After 1949, the intellectual diaspora among the KMT spoke to its floun-dering anatomy in Hong Kong and Taiwan as an owner might to a naughty

98   *Anatomies examined*

dog. The main worries were failure to develop proper habits or learn that unaccountability has bad outcomes. The prevailing climate of denial and blame shifting could not be understood to have future costs. Intellectuals demanded that the self-seeking failures were presented as clear historical footnotes to its anatomy, as if balance should be a feature of anatomy or that its remaining power centre of warlords with nowhere to go, and gun and drug-running Godfathers, worried about the rebuke of history or even occasionally thought about their image in such terms.

The futility of seeking a compromise Chinese government drove the retraction of remnant KMT forces to Taiwan, and made its suicidal terror raids on the Chinese mainland inevitable. The KMT militants were a bigger liability than an asset to the British in Hong Kong because their every act confirmed a strain of historical depression, an indifference to fate and a readiness to fight and resist mainland communism for not much more reason than American willingness to fund it. Its democratic, freedom-loving anatomy was broken beyond repair. The British were thinking about dignity in the face of their oblivion, and nothing else.

Comparing how and why each system made an individual take necessary actions or steps to reform is not to make a case that the systems were regularly alike. Rather, the ways in which each system attempted to limit or reform individuals without killing them or ensnaring them in barbed wire were always about control of who benefitted from a distribution of proceeds arising from the development of technical prowess. The definition of prowess ruled the efforts of some people valuable, and those of others suspicious or worthless.

Notes

1 Prasenjit Duara, 'Provincial Narratives of the Nation: Centralism and Federalism in Republican China' in Harumi Befu (ed), *Cultural Nationalism in East Asia: Representation and Identity* (Berkeley: Institute of East Asian Studies, 1993), 32.
2 Walter Laqueur, *No End to War: Terrorism in the Twenty-first Century* (New York: Continuum, 2004), 22.
3 Paul Wilkinson, 'Pathology and Theory' in Walter Laqueur (ed), *The Terrorism Reader: A Historical Anthology* (London: Wildwood House, 1979), 237.
4 Frank Dikötter, *The Age of Openness: China Before Mao* (Los Angeles: University of California, 2008).
5 Witold Rodzinski, *The People's Republic of China: A Concise Political History* (New York: Free Press, 1989), 47.
6 Rodzinski, 47.
7 Christine Loh, *Underground Front: The Chinese Communist Party in Hong Kong* (Hong Kong: Hong Kong University Press, 2010), 69.
8 Dikötter, 7.

9 HKRS 163-1-2029: 'Chau Yuen Szi to Secretary, Riot Compensation Advisory Board'.

10 HKRS 163-1-2029: 'Chau Yuen Szi'.

11 John Young, 'The Building Years: Maintaining a China-Hong Kong-Britain Equilibrium, 1950–1971' in Ming Chan (ed), *Precarious Balance Hong Kong Between China and Britain 1842–1992* (Hong Kong: Hong Kong University Press, 1994), 136.

12 Hu Sheng, *Imperialism and Chinese Politics* (Peking: Foreign Languages Press, 1955), 304.

13 Hu, 41.

14 Hu, 41.

15 HKRS 163-1-2029 (523/57/58): 'Communist Accounts'.

16 CIA-RDP82-00457R006200710001-8: 'Chinese Communist Message to Refugees in Hong Kong' (15 November 1950), 1.

17 Editorial, "Overseas Chinese" *Ta Kung Pao* (28 January 1950), 7.

18 CIA-RDP82-00457R006200710001-8: 'Chinese Communist Message'.

19 CIA-RDP82-00457R006200710001-8: 'Chinese Communist Message'.

20 CIA-RPD80-00809A000600380129-7: 'Communist Authorities in Northeast and North China Step Up Drive to Smash Counterrevolutionary Activity' (26 February 1951).

21 CIA-RPD80-00809A000600380129-7: 'Communist Authorities'.

22 CIA-RPD80-00809A000600380129-7: 'Communist Authorities'.

23 CIA-RPD80-00809A000600380129-7: 'Communist Authorities'.

24 CIA-RPD80-00809A000600380129-7: 'Communist Authorities'.

25 CIA-RDP82-00457R008000290002-4: 'Chinese Communist Terrorist Activities in the Hong Kong/Kowloon Area' (17 August 1951).

26 CIA-RDP82-00457R008000290002-4: 'Chinese Communist Terrorist Activities'.

27 Jean Chesneaux, *Peasant Revolts in China 1840–1949* (London: Thames and Hudson, 1973), 165.

28 Lucien Bianco, *Origins of the Chinese Revolution 1915–1949* (Stanford: Stanford University Press, 1967), 27–52.

29 Bianco, 166.

30 HKRS163-1-2029 (523/57/58): 'Communist Accounts': 'HK & Kowloon Spinning, Weaving and Dyeing Trade Workers General Union' (14 September 1957), 1.

31 HKRS163-1-2029 (523/57/58), 'Communist Accounts', 2.

32 HKRS163-1-2029 (523/57/58): 'Communist Accounts', 2.

33 HKRS163-1-2029 (523/57/58): 'Extract From Press Summaries' Dated 12 September 1957.

34 HKRS163-1-2029 (523/57/58): 'Communist Accounts'.

35 HKRS163-1-2029 (523/57/58): 'Communist Accounts'.

36 HKRS163-1-2029 (523/57/58): 'Communist Accounts'.

37 CIA-RDP82-00457R005200230008-5: 'Kuomintang Attempts to Nullify Third Party Movements' (11 July 1950), 1.

38 CIA-RDP82-00457R005200230008-5: 'Kuomintang Attempts'.

39 CIA-RDP82-00457R005200230008-5: 'Kuomintang Attempts'.

40 CIA-RDP82-00457R005200230008-5: 'Kuomintang Attempts'.

41 CIA-RDP82-00457R005200230008-5: 'Kuomintang Attempts'.

42 HKRS 184-4-4-4/ CO 537/1658: 'Kuomintang Activities 1946–1951' (File:18 June 1946).
43 HKRS 184-4-4-4: 'Kuomintang Activities'.
44 HKRS 184-4-4-4: 'Kuomintang Activities'.
45 HKRS 184-4-4-4: 'Kuomintang Activities'.
46 HKRS 184-4-4-4: 'Facts about Mr Shumwaiyau'.
47 HKRS 184-4-4-4: 'File: P.L. Radford' (24 July 1948).
48 HKRS184-4-4-4: 'Facts about Mr Shumwaiyau'.
49 HKRS184-4-4-4: 'Facts about Mr Shumwaiyau'.

5   Orthodoxy

Introduction

This final chapter positions orthodoxy as an always-tensile bridge between anatomy and underlying ontologies of communism and colonialism. Orthodoxy – in my reading – was a state of plausibility and indeterminate as to success or failure. It takes the form of a liveable compromise, but is as characteristic of the state as its anatomy or a covered-over ontology. This chapter puts the southern China iteration of British colonialism alongside Chinese nationalism in its communist form to argue that discord and patchy accommodation – rather than an expectation of dialectical synthesis – best assists the telling of colonial and communist histories. The British colonial regime in Hong Kong could be expected to put its anatomy forward as an indisputable account of events. Communists could be expected to refute it. Hence, strategic horse-trading between ideological exponents needs to take centre stage rather than histories of mutual influence or separatism.

It will be recalled that, in 1956, Whitehall made a complaint to the Chinese communists on their perceived over-reaction at attribution of riot blame. The British government accused the CCP of 'attempts to inflame the situation by such exaggerated reports'[1] and hoped 'in the future the Chinese press would show greater restraint and greater regard for the facts'.[2] This was rebuffed by the Chinese vice-minister for foreign affairs (Zhang Hangfu), who asked whether 'the Hong Kong authorities would change their attitude of shielding and conniving with Kuomintang who threatened the mainland and created disturbances in Hong Kong?'[3]

The Chinese vice-minister refused to assume responsibility for the left-wing press in Hong Kong. This was on grounds that:

> if the Hong Kong authorities assumed responsibility for punishing KMT agents and if they maintained law and order, the press would report it' but, having regard to the unconvincing British position

during and after the riot, 'it was natural and reasonable for the Chinese people to express their indignation'.[4]

The view of the Secretary of State for the Commonwealth was that 'the riots must be such a satisfactory development from the point of view of the Chinese government' and, with a resigned tone, suggested that 'it would be surprising if they did not make political capital out of them'.[5]

The separatism in both communist and colonial accounts of history tended to link intellectualism with historical revisionism and pursuit of an inappropriate distribution of gains from modernity. Each side wanted to remember a particular history and limit access to technological advantage to a special set of true believers. This was why unsupervised intellectual activity could only lead to a power base for anti-orthodox political formations. It also revealed the importance of accretions of improvement making nostalgia a determined political belief with ways of measuring its claims. Colonialism resorted first to an instinctive credo of ruthless exclusion in the sense that proximity to trademarks counted one into or out of professional opportunity and the dividends of ownership. Assured domination of a progress mechanism could be easily disrupted by scientific developments enabling better results for a wider benefit, and the revised productive monopoly this implied.

Chinese communists took control over production, and its improvement, for a presumptive wider benefit in 1949. They had no equivalent of the monopolist leap-frogging in a colonial or foreign-dominated Chinese system, and had a social ordering system unconnected to invention and distribution of gleaming machines. A problem for Red thinking lay not in the establishment or revisions in industrial monopoly – they had that all to themselves. It was finding a way to ensure waves of successor technology continued to come close together once the West and its exclusive club were swept out of the way after 1949. This is why the orthodoxy – an anatomy with a grounding in some reality – in my account of Chinese communism was not about the tension between technical expertise and Yen'an principles. It was about exploring new ways of national development outside of the cursed industrial realm and immature limitations of communist cultural products. The CCP's early Hong Kong experience was not only an anatomical conflict of playing landlords on one side of the border and purging them on the other side, but one of indulging buy-and-sell capitalism in as close to a spirit of play as its weary solemnity would allow in 1950.

This chapter raises the impervious and unifying qualities of state ideological orthodoxy in the cases of British East Asian colonialism and Chinese communism. Communists sought to limit the externality of human rights entering their political exchanges, and colonial capitalists usually rooted out class-based collectivism inspired by communism. Such treatment of opposition has been a frequent cause for a critique of communism. However, seldom has liberalism's battle with its enemy within been framed as an indictment of the whole system. The generally live-and-let-live approach of Hong Kong authorities to Chinese communism must be regarded as at least a partial achievement of liberal orthodoxy.

Communism and colonial capitalism were under constant threat from externalities that had no purpose other than to challenge state power by lowering their anatomy. This chapter concludes the book with a few remarks about the prevailing commentary on the discomfort caused to China by human rights questions. Widely broadcast Chinese material progress – absent a framework of human rights – has been converted by indifferent trading relationships into the intractable destiny of all parties to international diplomacy.

Orthodoxy and technical knowledge

The ability of Chinese communists to assume representation of the Chinese people and speak on their behalf in colonial or home country contexts depended on what Lifton identified as a claim to purity that dominated 'Red thinking'.[6] It placed greater value on narrowly measuring the consistency of similar political ideas for their uprightness rather than expounding on constitutional differences between China and elsewhere in a spirit of openness. The term 'Red thinking' was used by CCP leaders themselves, and it stood in for religious faith. By the early 1960s, it symbolised a concern that if CCP members were 'a bit slack' in political and ideological work, then economic and technical efforts 'will surely go astray'.[7]

In Red thinking, nothing other than a literal interpretation of art was necessary. Orthodoxy flattened in order to broaden, but it had mixed success. Chinese communist art critics seldom had much to say. In the Chinese communist tradition from the mid-1950s to the mid-1960s, literature, film and other cultural products either held passion and boldness, and risked a label of revisionism in their pursuit of individualistic freedom, or unambiguously served a proletarian constituency whose historical moment of civilisation had come, even if cadre-status was needed to feel its full benefit. Orthodoxy's leaden effect on art showed up elsewhere, including the ambitions and outputs of factories. Industry freely supplied needs such as enamelled bowls. Chromium-plated pens and valve radios were 'wants'. They were quite special because they indicated status in a nation priding itself on there being no better jobs, just different ones.

The One Hundred Flowers campaigns of 1957 and 1961–1962, and later, the Cultural Revolution, drove a hunt for restoration records to prove cases of divergent intellectualism or technical development that did not advance Red thinking, or its projects of extending bicycle ownership and civic virtue combatting indifference. Yet for all the social chaos such anti-intellectual movements caused, they were motivated by a genuine belief that Chinese people could improve their standard of living and join modernity by themselves, by starting afresh, and do so on their own terms. The colonial ghost was freely invoked. Chinese people, so went Red thinking, did not need Western liberal permission to be good enough for their own country. A large part of Red thinking rested on the rejection of Western culture. As late as the mid-1980s, a popular communist Chinese term of censure was to refer to someone a 'Westernised freak'. There is the steady gaze of a predatory animal inside those words.

Representations of a colonial mindset were based on orthodoxies of the deserving civilised as an immutable group. The colonial consensus about wider access to dividends of modernity regarded it as a goal for the future. Colonialism stressed that constitutionalism was designed for some people, but not others. Local conditions had to be raised before local people could be considered to bear rights in the way of a European. The anatomy depicted by colonial literature and film pitted solipsistic white heroism against an alleged tendency of locals to clannish backsliding. This legitimated restriction of suffrage to those obviously capable of participating in the dominant nexus of constitutional selection and technical progress. This was proclaimed a natural law, although colonial romanticism preached rather more to the converted than did communist idealised realism. The CCP implied that political power was available through an individual's absorption of its prescribed thinking and conduct. Such a good offer had to be repeated a lot because 'the mass line' was intended for everyone; in fact, it was designed for the indifferent.

Lifton has no peer in his probing of the causes of communist Chinese anxiety about intellectualism. He framed it as the preference for being 'Red' rather than 'expert'.[8] In this light, 'the people' held 'the special revolutionary combination of purity and power [which] could in itself completely nourish the individual mind', making 'any additional intellectual needs . . . suspect.'[9] He identified in Maoist policy a strong line against 'restorationist impulse'.[10] It embodied 'true Chinese' as those rural and close to the earth, and urban Chinese as somewhat contaminated and foreign.[11] To be a communist was to aim to be literate but not expert, and part of a government of amateurs bent on abolishing what Mao termed 'the old learning'.[12] Hence, for Mao, the political revolution in China lay in constantly turning over of positions of power within a trusted framework of Red ideas. This posed no problem about who to salvage from the past. Which 'new learning'[13] could be a front-facing example of Red orthodoxy was a more difficult question to answer because it had to pass through anti-feudalism and anti-imperialism filters.

The idea of elites blocking access to technical advantage in the productive means was not really new to the CCP. China had been governed by the elites of Old Society formations that stood in for colonialism as an equivalence or a proxy. Education and technical expertise were jealously guarded islands in that pre-1949 world. As the CCP gained momentum in the mid-1930s, a core of believers, as Chesneaux recognised, comprised of a composition of urbanites, left-wing army men, intellectuals and rural workers who had bivouacked with the PLA, began to envisage a different China.[14] After victory in the civil war, a critique developed among uneducated men and women who held positions of political power. Remnants of the Old Society who had suppressed educational opportunity of the masses were deemed to have complicated backgrounds that made them unsuitable for political roles or improvement by marriage or university life or any further means to social advancement. A significant element of Red orthodoxy relied on enforcing restrictions on the old enemy in such ways. This was easily procured proof that the victorious anatomy of the people's revolution matched its reality. Victory and liberation brought new opportunity to the core of believers. Red thinking could be seen as a plausible orthodoxy outside technical or artistic domains.

The enforcement of Red orthodoxy did not rely only on promoting the right sort of people. It had a territorial aspect too. A trait shared by colonialism and communism, it mattered little to call it 'defending the revolution' or 'gunboat diplomacy'. Mao's fatalism was based on his acceptance that history could not be stopped but only nudged at decisive points, and the symbolism of extinguishing separatism or middle-management empire building was crucial to Red orthodoxy. This was an idea that the Communist Party of the Soviet Union (CPSU) made clear when it claimed that crushing the uprising in Hungary in 1956 was 'the only correct course to take' and demonstrated 'our international duty'.[15] China approved of the CPSU's Hungary repression. The Russian observations originated in a political party that wished to defeat history and demonstrate itself eternally paramount:

> The dictatorship of the proletariat, once established, is committed to the use of necessary violence, unrestricted by law, in order to destroy the domestic enemy, to make counterrevolution impossible, and to defeat invasion from abroad.[16]

The annihilationist instinct expressed in this quotation could be thought to distinguish communism from the colonial ethos, yet in 1956, it did not necessarily seem that way. Soviet leader Nikita Khrushchev's bad press for putting down the Hungarian revolution was nullified by widespread Western disdain for Anthony Eden's imperial folly in Egypt over the Suez conducted as if Britain still needed a dedicated military seaway to India. Defending territorial orthodoxy required timing and verve, and could never succeed if it looked like regression to too many people. When nothing happens after the assertion of territorial orthodoxy it is taken as confirmation and approval, just as it is when internal orthodoxy on a novel issue is voiced without dissent. Orthodoxy, whatever its ideological stripe, had to be plausible to resist push-back and convenient to historical narration. This did not make its exponent a great historian or overly concerned for the demographic proof of happiness.

Colonial modernity

For colonialists, their assumption of racial superiority at the root of many of their actions – conscious and otherwise – could not be made explicit to the people that they ruled. Not that colonials were concerned about the humiliation of 'the natives'. Rather, no colonialist wanted to renounce the upper hand in tensions caused by nation and technology existing between them and their 'native' enemies. Doing so, or relying too heavily on the comparison of race, would call into question what Marshall anointed as 'a deliberate, sustained and self-conscious attempt to order an imperial community in the image of society at home'.[17] Prevailing social subjugations would be weakened by explicitly alluding to racial barriers as crucial to ruling the colonial moment, or its project of aloofly replicating home. Much safer, in most cases, to let technology imply superiority and to quarantine access to its production dividends.

A maudlin colonial suspicion took it for granted that locals habitually used knowledge gaps to take advantage of colonisers. Such guardedness cramped nearly every colonial soul. In the ghoulish imaginary of George MacDonald Fraser in *Flashman and the Dragon*, this point could not go without being made: 'Delay. Chinese talk. Can't have it. Drive on. Don't give 'em time to scheme. Treacherous fellows'.[18] Learning the local language was ambivalently fobbed off as eccentric behaviour. Yet, as Fraser at least realised, colonial cultural illiteracy indebted European traders to locals out East.

The profits of technology quarantine for foreigners were reduced by the translation expenses of parlay. The colonial anatomy referred to superior technology as giving a prerogative to govern. Bringing civilisation without necessarily sharing a technical or intellectual advantage was a disjointed and disreputable project. Such trickster tactics prepared China's communists perfectly for eventual victory. It prepared them to govern, too.

The essential parasitism of colonial thinking meant that it preached to the converted and economically marginalised everyone who could not be rounded up and set to its economic purpose. Using labour migration to create a curtain of ethnic conflict around the economic purpose of colonialism were its realities, as was technology quarantine, but neither carried a transformative prospect for most people. In China, the Taiping episode had taught colonial powers that civil war created economic chaos and uncertainty for them. Colonialism had to distribute a fraction of its dividend to its host jurisdiction as a kind of protection payment. Without it, the anatomy began to look rather suspect because its private purpose was open to direct inspection. No technology could out-compete compradorial commercial know-how at the gateway of a market. European racial destiny, and developmental anatomy, found special challenges in China along such lines.

Dangers of relaxation

If Red thinking enjoyed mixed success on the industrial front, where could it make its mark? As Lifton recognised, the communist leadership of the 1950s cared less about the revolution 'falling into the hands of a different leader' than 'the new leader espousing an alternative – and therefore impure – revolutionary vision'.[19] Communist correspondent in China Ku Feng argued that comrades should not watch movies for the 'sake of relaxation', but if young people 'were not influenced by the proletarian ideology' of Chinese films in the late 1960s, they 'will be exposed to bourgeois ideology . . . undermining our revolutionary will'.[20] In a six-page rejoinder, the editor of *China Youth* conceded that 'a few comrades' believed 'some films made in our country, reflecting the struggle on the industrial and agricultural fronts, are not of very high artistic standard and therefore are not inclined to see such films.'[21] In his reply he further contended:

> Not only should young people of the new China seek constant replenishment and enhancement in work and study, but they should also cultivate good taste during rest and recreation periods by accepting Communist education through literary and artistic appreciation while watching movies and rejecting the influence of modern revisionist and bourgeois ideas.[22]

The sayings of Chairman Mao could not constitute the whole of an individual's thoughts. Watching movies for relaxation was how bourgeois culture slipped into vulnerable minds and cut the tether of an individual to the political struggle and the ongoing demands of the revolution. The denouncement of hundreds of thousands of China's intellectuals as 'Rightist' in 1957 following the failed One Hundred Flowers campaign, according to Alexander, showed that 'many intellectuals had not abandoned Western liberal concepts and were willing to criticise the Communist system itself'.[23]

The communist message came from the bottom and moved upwards. The CCP put its faith in worthy films inspiring a can-do attitude among the levelled masses. If the plot of *The East is Red* impressed its audience: 'members of a Peking suburban commune hurdle obstacles and successfully grow their own vegetables under the leadership of the Party',[24] then *Streams of Water, Songs of Joy* must surely have invoked their rapture: 'on peasants building their own hydro-electric station and the growth of technical experts among the peasantry'.[25]

For communists, the point of films was not to relax, but to be instructed. Only by being permanently on 'transmit' could bourgeois, capitalist ideas be faced down by communism. The demons and animal spirits assuming human form in the classic novel *Journey to the West* easily became European industrialists encountered in China's slow journey to modernisation – motivated by strange forces and evasive about how their machines worked. Co-operation with such strange creatures seemed unthinkable. They were treated as one might treat a target of espionage. One's guard had to be up. If these white devils achieved their purpose, one was apt to be swept away on a tide of coffee and commercial laws that seemed to equivocate about who wins.

The long tradition of Chinese anti-foreignism lay in mercantilist protectionism. At the point, however, when it no longer protected China, the communists assumed control and began making choices from the scanty options left by foreign futurism. This is why communist films about self-sufficiency and enlisting the help of technical experts from Russia were not regarded as contradictory. It was about having a Red reason to pluck at whatever was needed by the country. The slippery evils of Western culture lay in its self-absorption. Films that one reflected on for personal meanings could lead to expressing ideas that endangered social harmony, and gave no-one an enamelled pot.

Human rights and the new imperialism

Flip open almost any history of Hong Kong and the old fictions are many and easy to spot. Governors are assumed to have always had the last say. The British were benign rulers walking a tightrope of extremisms. Seeing this, the Chinese population of Hong Kong maintained their refugee mindset and, abstaining from politics, worked tirelessly under British governance to deny oxygen to unhelpful politics and make Hong Kong a fabulous success. The communists had no real sway in the affairs of the colony, etc., etc.

No narrative seeks to explain the experience of Hong Kong in terms of the post-colonial transition of the United Kingdom, or the discomforting seasonal allegiances that made it possible. The British colonial administration could not contend to Chinese nationalists that 'violence was never the answer' because an imperial power had to formally leave its colonies and airbrush its historiography in order to champion modern human rights – albeit that the Americans never treated this as an impediment.

Those historians in the KMT Three who want to critique the old communist brutalities need to do more than take the horizon of Old Society politics as an unspoken motive to study history. The victors and their princely progeny in today's Politburo – all of them – have a single version of history rarely responded to by the historians of the West. Even with the best will in the world, no dialectical result can come from a one-sided process of listening for evil and fearlessly recognising virtue. There must be a battle of antithetical ideas. That has to be better than the sonorous judgment and sour rebuke of every historian who takes the ethics of Western constitutional humanism as their inspiration for China history studies.

After the Second World War, Western victors scrambled to the lectern to evangelise to the East on the dangers of arbitrary government to newly won human rights. In the case of China, they demonstrated a misplaced confidence that communist rights could be seen as a passing fad; or that its askew picture frame could be easily straightened. This was coupled with their unrelenting desire to re-colonise China, not perhaps territorially, but by remaking her in their own distorted image through the calculated side-effects of trade. A communist front organisation that established offices in Shanghai and Hong Kong in 1947, the so-called 'International Society for the Defence of Human Rights', had as part of its platform both the 'establishment of a free and liberal China' and 'to have American forces withdrawn from China'.[26]

The sincerity of the Society was a much less important question than its idea that the rights agenda in China did not take its cues from Western influences. After the Sino-Russian split, China was described by the Americans in 1977 as 'the only communist country that has derived some satisfaction from the US [human rights] stand'.[27] Yet the Chinese communists enjoying the berating Russia received over human rights abuses was interpreted by the Americans as masking their 'private misgivings' about 'their vulnerability on the human rights issue'[28] disclosed by their media-shy approach to reporting the U.S.-Russia human rights controversy. The CIA freely admitted that, in the communist world, there was 'a notable reluctance to accept the US stand at face value' and suspicion of 'human rights as a ploy designed to pressure other countries into comporting themselves in accordance with US policies generally'.[29] In 1947 or 1977, the CCP's approach remained consistent: China's hard-won sovereignty from Western influence was endangered by the U.S.-sponsored human rights agenda.

Communist Chinese paranoia about the progress of the revolution and its purity has so many historical grounds that it can be regarded as a legitimate suspicion guiding many aspects of its policy. The Western concoction of human rights critique can only be seen in such a light. The communist historical model drew strength, in dealing with emerging challenges such as human rights, from viewing them in Red terms. It did not need imported expertise to understand the interface of citizen and state.

China's economic liberalisation over the last four decades has not implied a dilution of Red purity and power. Nor has its gradual shift from the archetypes of the country to the city resulted in a widespread notice of a historical contradiction. The communist Chinese put hard work into history. Arguably, economic advancement in China has not been a discussion about individuals, yet elevating a concept of community that no longer exists in China to a position of state policy is at odds with the free-for-all of modern urban China. An individual in China is politically conceived as inseparable from others but allowed to line their own pockets – hence the political punch attributed to anti-corruption charges. That would be a clever shift if it were not so diabolical. The reality underneath the Chinese capitalist anatomy is the highest conditionality imaginable to a human life. An individual is limitless – except in the case of reaching an undisclosed arbitrary point.

These days, almost no hope exists of the old human rights idealists playing any role in an upright future for a bourgeois Chinese democracy. The 'Charter 08' movement included separation of powers, independent judiciary and election of public officials as anti-graft measures. The subversive yearning for scrubbed democrats has seldom been stronger. Rather, it is the use of 'decay' by the Chartists to describe the current communist system, along with the human restriction and indignity it is alleged to preside over, that prevents democratic reform in the vein of a new federal republican state.[30] What is occurring in the Chinese communist system is not decay, but defended ossification. Arbitrary arrest, detention and punishment do not 'rot away the humanity of people',[31] as 'Charter 08' suggests. They protect historical political asymmetries and princeling privilege in ways that no self-respecting communist government could otherwise defend.

The Chinese Communist Party of today has created a winning class of property developers, desecrating industrialists and municipal 'yes men' and a losing class of lawyer-less, mopey petitioners who mistakenly believe that economic rights in New China include refusing to move out of the hutong for an apartment or a crumbling cave village for a new town. These people and their children, spread wide by the internal diaspora, are at the pointy end of economic change in China, making them the first obvious constituency of a Charter-based democracy movement in China. If human rights are economic rights, as the CCP constantly claims, make the party live up to it for the sake of millions of people left behind in the new China of landlords, rather than dream of creating another bourgeois democracy with a penumbra of media-star human rights enjoyed by a handful of people. Chartists could start by promoting unity among those experiencing vulnerability and dislocation created by economic development, and let its embarrassing implication for the historical objectives of the CCP go viral.

A communist's account of China's history relies on identifying 'the people' and governing them according to representative prescriptions. Commentators tend to roll their eyes at Beijing's frequent accusation that a company, individual or nation state has been guilty of 'hurting the feelings of the Chinese people'.[32] It does come across a little precious. However, it is unclear why this imagining of state power has been regarded in the West a less representative version of history than those expounded by any of the proto-liberal parties from which the CCP wrenched power. The KMT Three show quick concern for the deaths of millions as though their colonial proxies did not understand that the fight for China was going to be a fight to the death careless of human rights, or did not appreciate that in such a fight, only extinguishment of the other side would guarantee victory. Such revisionism has become rampant among China scholars of the West these days.

The brutal over-reaction among communist cadres, soldiers and guards toward reactionary saboteurs can be regarded as a symptom of the revolution's vulnerability, even among its most fervent exponents. Communist apparatchik Peng Cheng, Deputy Chairman of the Political and Law Committee of the Administrative Council, explained it in absolutist terms developed over two decades of the see-saw struggle with the KMT: 'if we do not thoroughly destroy the people's enemy, there cannot be a people's victory. To be lenient and magnanimous is to be cruel to the people'.[33] This could be suspected as promoting a sentimental regard for the sacrifices of communist supporters. They were not to be dishonoured by going lightly on the old enemy. It also seems to accept that humane treatment and rehabilitation of some nationalists into the communist system was impossible, even after party membership was allowed to swell with newcomers after 1945.

Conclusion including chapter summaries

Chapter 1 showed that the CCP appreciated the commercial calm of the Hong Kong during the first half of the 1950s, and pursued an anti-capitalist purge policy on home soil at the same time. This fractured its anatomy, making it capitalist in Hong Kong and anti-capitalist at home. Foreign exchange access, indirect materials acquisition for the Korean War and the rules-based commercial stability of Hong Kong were factors favourable enough for them not to invade the colony, particularly throughout the early 1950s. Although notional commercial equality was enjoyed by KMT members and communists using the colony, this was disfigured badly by the British administration not checking Hong Kong's use by the KMT as a base for reprisal and sabotage raids by KMT remnant militants throughout the 1950s. The United Front pursued by Zhou Enlai in the colony was generally a shoe-string affair depending on fanning discontent in a time of water shortages, indiscriminate police actions or price shocks. Communist resistance to colonialism was expressed in reality in 1957 and 1967. The United Front would briefly include British colonialism in 1963.

Chapter 1 also observed that the colonial anatomy maintained equal business opportunity existed for communists and KMT figures if they abided by the laws of the colony. Yet this supposed impartiality did not extend to the colonial administration bringing KMT extremists to heel in the colony or preventing their violent behaviour in mainland China. They had *carte blanche* in Hong Kong, and sensible businessmen with KMT-gangster affiliations not waving the flag too much were preferred commercial partners of the British – something proven by riot compensation records. These operators were the Old China grandees of the KMT. At least they had good manners – something that mattered greatly to the British as a gauge to character and intention. The communists did not believe in friendship or manners. By giving accurate intelligence missives, they expected prompt action from the British colonial administration. This they first received in 1963.

Chapter 2 presented the case of Leung Tong as an example of how the denial of ordinary compensation claims formed part of a ruse to allocate guilt as a non-political criminality of bystanders and communists and to compensate big KMT losses in the riot opaquely. There was a range of questions not answered satisfactorily in the case that suggest an extraordinary compensative reality lay beneath the thin colonial carapace.

There is next to no likelihood that Mr Leung was a KMT agent, or one of its opportunist street thugs cloaking opportunism in a banned flag. Either status would have conferred on him a measure of immunity. His widow's fight was squarely against a colonial presumption that her husband was an opportunist property criminal – a status it was safe to accord him because he was not sufficiently political. The colonial state merely played out its assigned role of hoarding its pennies for compensating people who returned its favours.

The period reviewed in this book was largely a period of territorial integrity and early confidence in the communist republic of China. After the Korean offensive started in the middle of 1950, the nation's leadership was mostly interested in consolidating its gains by pumping inexperienced troops and turbulent generals into the north, rather than picking a fight on the southern border that was neither strictly necessary and, in the case of Hong Kong, would compromise the indirect communist war materials procurement bound for Korea. By 1963, however, none of the old geopolitical reasons existed to make the communists go quietly in Hong Kong.

Hong Kong was viewed by the CCP as a haven for KMT counter-revolutionaries at the very time the PLA forces were trying to consolidate their control over the country. The uprisings and rebellions by ex-KMT factions in southern China were seen as being partly fuelled by the Rightist ambivalence of the British in Hong Kong. The British were pursuing the future of the colony by currying up to big businessmen, and the Communist Chinese saw their efforts to bring their country under control being eroded by the British administration. This finally changed in 1963.

Chapter 3 showed how the British were, by their own admission, compelled to work more closely with the communists to prosecute KMT militants in 1963. The partnership of the U.S. State Department and the KMT waned over time. The Americans had a crisis of confidence in the KMT being able to carry out anti-communist missions in southern China without embroiling it in disputes with third-party states.

The British colonial administration preferred the commercial dynamism of the refugee business elements of the KMT, and its ability along with U.S. support, to back post-1949 militant action in mainland China. In the colonial mind, the doleful soliloquies of the Chinese communists on British responsibilities to Chinese people in the colony came a distant second for most of the 1950s. The KMT's post-civil war sabotage raids in southern China expressed the lax colonial policing of the border or law and order in Hong Kong. It was amended only after a steady stream of Chinese communist complaints from 1956 to 1962. This briefly appeased the communists and cast an eye to the future relationship. For the rest of the 1960s, the British were finally thrust into a mode of colonial invigilation against KMT militarist remnants.

Chapters 4 and 5 found that the anatomies of Chinese communist, bourgeois Chinese and colonial nationalism each made a structural conclusion about the relationship of orthodox thinking within its tradition and the proper distribution of modernity's advantages. Thus, if one made the focus of history about the tension between an anatomy's promise and its realisation, the anatomies of British colonialism and bourgeois Chinese republicanism each wore exceedingly thin as a credible explanation for actual state actions. The communist anatomy only maintained a degree of integrity by lowering human expectation to make a poorly rewarded life in public service and entertainment based on instruction its highest goals. The communist anatomy suffered from mixed messaging when it spoke to expatriate Chinese. Its foray into the capitalism of Hong Kong made it an early example of what would become a post-Deng norm, but a conflicted one at the time, especially its position on landlords.

The cases of Leung Tong (Ho Mo Ching) and Chau Yuen Szi raised a question of whether standing outside of the three nationalist anatomies of the 1950s was a viable position. Mao ventured a view that people cannot be called communists if they 'make some small contribution . . . swell with pride and brag about it for fear that others will not know'.[34] Under communism, ordinary working people changed the world with unrecognised hard work. Under colonialism, hard work was also unrecognised, but 'the people' was not its object. When Kafka reflected on who constructed the Great Wall, he came to Mao's conclusion about the quiet builders but would have disagreed with the Great Helmsman that they were an admired force in politics: 'innocent northern people believed that they were the cause; the admirable innocent emperor believed he had given orders for it. We who are builders of the wall know otherwise and are silent'.[35]

A philosophical prospect is raised that under colonial capitalism or communism, a third force beyond leadership constructed the new world, sewed sorghum, levelled building sites, dragged sodden wooden fishing boats up the beach, heaved into coal into the furnaces, dug the irrigation ditches, etc. Such people knew an immunity to politics that would see a reactionary or a bandit given work as punishment. These were the people of Lao Tzu: 'laying no claim to merit was why merit never left them'.[36] Such people exist everywhere, mutely observing an anatomy struggling to raise an official explanation of a setback that would be all the deeper for them not going to work. They did not believe a word of an anatomy – communist, bourgeois nationalist or colonial. But it did not really matter to their ruler. Mao was wrong. The quiet toilers existed insular from their rhetorical cartoon and outside the politics of acclaim.

Let it be said that Mr Leung did not lightly abandon selling flouncy skirts of gingham and satin on Friday afternoon to go steal a radiogram before curfew. Let him be a man who traipsed home having fallen ill after a morning of attentive service. Let Mrs Chau be imagined not as the mother of a wild boy buried in a secret place. Picture her spending her morning in a line of women heaving water buckets up mouldy tenement stairs so that her family could drink, wash and be clean when she received news of her son being slain, in her eyes, as an innocent in an alleyway of the riot. Both colonial and communist systems laid their claim to the same souls.

Colonialism in Hong Kong usually invested in its 'model native', but unlike communism in China, made limited use of their model's exemplary powers beyond veneration of Eurasian business acumen. Colonialism did not situate itself – quixotic – alongside its subjects, as communism purported to do, but above them. It carried a God-ordained trust, or in the vocabulary of this text, a didactic anatomy that constructed a place for everything and put everything in its place, according to ownership of the latest machines.

After their experiences, Mr Leung, together with his widow, Ho Mo Ching, and Mrs Chau, could not have believed either communism or colonial capitalism were a vehicle for the good in human nature. Such people became misshapen by tensing up and recoiling at the moment when their potential seemed most possible. They were people who raised a question about innocence at the very moment they realised it was not worth asking. They had become one of Kafka's selfless southern builders of the Great Wall. They had not lived their lives hoping that colonialism or communism would name them as models.

Party members in the politics of China were never allowed to discover that there was no place to go. A republican revolutionary slipped into the gangster life. A communist bandit in the hills became a village chairperson. By not holding prescribed enemy status per se, or toiling with recognition, the Ho Mo Chings and Chau Yuen Szis were consoled by their freedom from a political party. In places such as southern China and Hong Kong in the 1950s where organised pettiness – not revolution – prevailed, the confirmation of their souls as unworthy made them strong in an imagination of happiness.

Notes

1 HKMS 158-3-1: 'Telegram 4: Secretary of State for the Commonwealth Alan Lennox-Boyd to Sir A. Grantham' (20 October 1956), [4].
2 HKMS 158-3-1, 'Telegram 4', [5].
3 HKMS 158-3-1, 'Telegram 4', [6].
4 HKMS 158-3-1, 'Telegram 4', [6].
5 HKMS 158-3-1: 'Telegram 5: Secretary of State for the Commonwealth to Sir A. Grantham' (20 October 1956), [3].
6 Robert Lifton, *Revolutionary Immortality: Mao Tse-tung and the Chinese Cultural Revolution* (London: Weidenfeld, 1968), 45.
7 Chen Yi's speech quoted in Bill Brugger, *China: Liberation and Transformation 1942–1962* (London: Croom Helm, 1981), 242–243.
8 Lifton, 53.
9 Lifton, 53.
10 Lifton, 54.
11 Lifton, 54.
12 Anne Freemantle (ed), *Mao Tse-tung: An Anthology of His Writings* (New York: Mentor, 1962), 186.

13 Freemantle, 186.
14 Jean Chesneaux, *Peasant Revolts in China 1840–1949* (London: Thames and Hudson, 1973), 107.
15 CIA-RDP78-00915R001300230001-1: 'Communist Theory on Use of Violence and Guerrilla Warfare' (28 March 1961), 15.
16 CIA-RDP78-00915R001300230001-1: 'Communist Theory'.
17 Peter Marshal cited in Goh Chor Boon, *Technology and Entrepot Colonialism in Singapore* (Singapore: Institute of South East Asian Studies, 2013), 243.
18 George MacDonald Fraser, *Flashman and the Dragon* (London: Harper Collins, 1999), 48.
19 Lifton, 65.
20 CIA-RDP80R01731R000400360002-1: 'Films in China' in 'CIA Bulletin' (7 December 1960), 4.
21 CIA-RDP80R01731R000400360002-1: 'Films in China'.
22 CIA-RDP80R01731R000400360002-1: 'Films in China'.
23 Bevin Alexander, *The Strange Connection: The U.S. Intervention in China 1944–1972* (New York: Greenwood Press, 1992), 168.
24 CIA-RDP80R01731R000400360002-1: 'Films in China'.
25 CIA-RDP80R01731R000400360002-1: 'Films in China'.
26 CIA-RDP83-00415R000200090029-8: 'Political Information: The International Society for the Defense of Human Rights' (24 February 1947).
27 CIA-RDP80R01362A000200100001-6: 'Impact of the U.S. Stand on Human Rights' (11 May 1977), 4.
28 CIA-RDP80R01362A000200100001-6: 'Impact', 4.
29 CIA-RDP80R01362A000200100001-6: 'Impact', 1–2.
30 Liu Xiaobo, 'In full: Charter 08 Liu Xiaobo's pro-democracy manifesto for China that led to his jailing' (14 July 2017) Avail. at: www.hongkongfp.com/2017/07/14/full-charter-08-liu-xiaobos-pro-democracy-manifesto-china-led-jailing/ (accessed: 29 March 2018).
31 Liu Xiaobo, 'In full: Charter 08'.
32 David Bandurski, 'Hurting the Feelings of the Zhao Family' Avail at: http://chinamediaproject.org/2016/01/29/hurting-the-feelings-of-the-zhao-family/ (accessed: 8 August 2018).
33 Robert Shaplen, 'Guerrillas – Our Hope in Red China' *Collier's* (21 July 1951), 13.
34 Mao, *Quotations from Chairman Mao Tse-tung* (London: Transworld Publishers, 1967), 136.
35 Franz Kafka, *The Great Wall of China: Stories and Reflections* (New York: Schocken Books, 1946), 4.
36 Lao Tzu, *Tao Te Ching* (London: Penguin Classics, 1963), 6.

References

Source notes taken by Rohan Price from HKRS/HKMS documents in the Hong Kong archive, Kwun Tong are available at: www.rohanprice.com/shared All the CIA documents relied on in this text can be found at: www.cia. gov/library/readingroom/

Archival

Public Records Office, Kwun Tong, Hong Kong

HKMS 158-1-283; CO1030/1605: Correspondence 'Mr Higham (Colonial Office) to Mr Pearce' (29 April 1963).
HKMS 158-1-283: 'Extract LIC Report for May'.
HKMS 158-1-283: 'Rt Hon Philip Noel-Baker M.P. to Nigel Fisher M.P.' (22 May 1963).
HKMS 158-1-283: 'HT Morgan (Commonwealth Office) to MacLehose (Foreign Office)' (23 May 1963).
HKMS 158-1-283: 'HT Morgan to M. MacLehose (Far Eastern Dept, Foreign Office)' (23 May 1963).
HKMS 158-1-283 CO1030/1605: Richard Hughes, 'Hong Kong Rounds up Formosa Spies' *Sunday Times* (9 June 1963).
HKMS 158-1-283 CO1030/1605: Telegram: 'Sir R Black to Secretary of State for the Colonies' (12 June 1963).
HKMS 158-1-283; CO1030/1605: 'The Chief Secretary E.G. Edward Willan to Higham, Commonwealth Office' (27 June 1963).
HKMS 158-1-283: 'EG Willan to CM MacLehose' (28 June 1963).
HKMS 158-1-283 CO1030/1605: 'Telegram 557 KMT Guerrillas: Sir R Black to Secretary of State for Commonwealth' (8 July 1963).
HKMS 158-1-283; CO1030/1605: Telegram: 'Sir R Black to Secretary of State for Commonwealth' (8 July 1963).
HKMS 158-1-283; CO 1030/1605: 'Telegram No 466: HM Consul Peking to Foreign Office' (13 July 1963).
HKMS 158-1-283: 'Quarterly L.I.C Report' (20 July 1963).
HKMS 158-1-283: Reuters Report: 'Saboteurs Have Been Working Through Hong Kong in Recent Months – Hau Sang Case' (30 July 1963).

HKMS 158-1-283: 'Sir R Black (Governor) to Secretary for State for Colonies' (31 July 1963).

HKMS 158-1-283; CO 1030/1605: 'MacLehose to EG Willan' (2 August 1963).

HKMS 158-1-283: Telegram: 'MacLehose (Foreign Office) to EG Willan (Chief Secretary)' (2 August 1963).

HKMS 158-1-283 CO1030/1605 Telegram: 'Sir R Black to Secretary of State for Commonwealth' (15 August 1963).

HKMS 158-1-283; CO1030/1605: 'KN Coates (Immigration and Nationality) to MacLehose (Foreign Office)' (3 September 1963).

HKMS 158-3-1: 'Telegram 1: O'Neil, Peking to FO' (16 October 1956).

HKMS 158-3-1: 'Telegram 3: Secretary of State for the Commonwealth Alan Lennox-Boyd to Sir A. Grantham' in 'Foreign Office Far Eastern Department 1954–6 Disturbances in Kowloon: Disturbances, Riots and Incidents' (20 October 1956).

HKMS 158-3-1 (440/01): 'Telegram 4: Secretary of State for the Commonwealth Alan Lennox-Boyd to Sir A. Grantham' (20 October 1956).

HKMS 158-3-1: 'Telegram 5: Secretary of State for the Commonwealth to Sir A. Grantham' (20 October 1956).

HKMS 158-3-1 (21/10/56): 'Sir A. Grantham to Secretary of State for the Commonwealth' (22 October 1956).

HKRS 158-3-1 (440/01): 'Telegram 2: Sir A Grantham to Secretary of State For Commonwealth' (22 October 1956).

HKRS 163-1-2029 (294/57); 3/811/57; 389/1459855; DFS(F) 23.4.58: 'Payment Arrangements for Riot Compensation'.

HKRS 163-1-2029: 'Chau Yuen Szi to Secretary, Riot Compensation Advisory Board'.

HKRS 163-1-2029 (523/57/58): 'Riot Compensation Report' (Cutting from SCMP) (28 August 1957).

HKRS163-1-2029/ 523/57/58: 'Communist Accounts': 'Workers Protest Against Riot Compensation' (clippings from *Ta Kung Pao* 31 August 1957).

HKRS 163-1-2029 (523/57/58): 'Extract From Press Summaries' (12 September 1957).

HKRS163-1-2029; 523/57/58: 'Communist Accounts': 'HK & Kowloon Spinning, Weaving and Dyeing Trade Workers General Union' (14 September 1957).

HKRS 163-1-2029: 'Deputy Colonial Secretary to Commissioner of Compensation' (18 September 1957).

HKRS 163-1-2029; 526/57/58: 'Communist Accounts': 'Hongkong Kowloon Chinese Farming and Agriculture Association to Colonial Secretary'.

HKRS 169-2-119: 'Following MacDougal for Wallinger' (undated).

HKRS 169-2-119: 'Telegram: NA Chungking to CIC Hong Kong' (6 October 1945).

HKRS 169-2-119: 'Telegram: State Officer (Intelligence) Hong Kong to Chief of Staff' (11 October 1945).

HKRS 169-2-119: 'Records Commander in Chief Hong Kong': 'Telegram: CIC Hong Kong to N.A. Chungking' (13 October 1945).

HKRS 184-4-21; 5/1162/48: 'Telegram: Government House Sir A. Grantham to A. Creech-Jones' (28 May 1948).

HKRS 184-4-21 (5/1162/48): 'Telegram: Government House A. Grantham to A. Creech Jones M.P.' (28 May 1948).

HKRS 184-4-21; 6/7761/1948: 'Kuomintang Activities': 'Telegram: Government House HK: A. Grantham to HBM Embassy Nanking' (24 June 1948).

HKRS 184-4-4-4: 'Facts about Mr Shumwaiyau'.

HKRS 184-4-4-4; CO 537/1658: 'Kuomintang Activities 1946–1951' (File: 18 June 1946).

HKRS 184-4-4-4 (6/761/48): 'Government House Hong Kong Sir A. Grantham to HBM Embassy Nanking' (24 June 1948).

HKRS 184-4-4-4: 'File: P.L. Radford' (24 July 1948).

HKRS 410-10-9: 'Riot Compensation Payments – Ex-Gratia Payments'.

PRO52562: 'Report Covering the Involvement of British and Gurkha Troops during the Civil Disturbances of 1956, 1966 and 1967' (British Forces, Post Office Hong Kong, 1987).

CIA

CIA-RDP75-B00380R000300080001-4: Frank Browning and Banning Garrett, 'The New Opium War' (5 January 1971) (unidentified magazine article cutting).

CIA-RDP75-00149R000400360002-0: 'Warren Unna, "Burma Gets Military Aid Unannounced"' (1 June 1961).

CIA-RDP78–00915R001300230001-1: 'Communist Theory on Use of Violence and Guerrilla Warfare' (28 March 1961).

CIA-RDP78–03061A000100020014–5: 'The Sino-Soviet Dispute as Seen by Pietro Nenni and the PSI' in 'Bi-weekly propaganda Guidance No. 53' (21 November 1960).

CIA-RDP79-R00904A000500020099-9: 'Memorandum for the Director, Validity of Present Estimate on Hong Kong SNIE 13–3–57, The Chinese Communist Threat to Hong Kong, date 19 November 1957' (16 February 1960).

CIA-RDP79-T00975A005400500001-6: 'Central Intelligence Bulletin' (28 December 1960).

CIA-RDP80–00809A000600300078-2: 'KMT Guerrillas Harass Southern Areas; Communists Arrest KMT agents in Peiping, Fu-Chou' (11 April 1950).

CIA-RDP80–00809A000600290205-2: 'KMT Special Agents, Guerrillas Active in Central Areas' (12 November 1950).

CIA-RDP80–00809A000600300662-3: 'KMT Guerrilla Attacks Increase in Kwangtung; CCF Warns Against KMT Agents' (2 May 1950).

CIA-RPD80–00809A000600320264-3: 'CCF Reports KMT Guerrilla Units Killed or Captured in Recent Campaigns' and 'Kwangsi Bandits Wiped Out' (Canton *Nan Fang Jih-pao*) (17 April 1950).

CIA-RDP80–00809A000600340704-2: 'KMT Agents Continue Sabotage' (17 July 1950).

CIA-RDP80–00809A000600350504-3: 'KMT Guerrilla Activities Continue in Various Localities' (18 October 1950).

CIA-RDP80–00809A000600360969-7: 'Communists Step up Shipping Service to Hong Kong 2. Foreign Ships Continue to Call Communist Ports' (18 December 1950).

CIA-RPD80–00809A000600380129-7: 'Communist Authorities in Northeast and North China Step Up Drive to Smash Counterrevolutionary Activity' (26 February 1951).

CIA-RDP80–00809A000600380626-5: 'Economic. Agriculture, Land Reform' translated excerpts from communist newspapers (30 March 1951).

CIA-RDP80–00810A001400600003–7: 'Chinese Communist Concentration Camps, Szechuan' (18 June 1953).

CIA-RDP80–00810A002600990007-8: '1. Fuel Oil Supplies, Communist China 2. Shipment of Refrigerators 3. J.K. Willy and Co, Hong Kong' (22 October 1953).

CIA-RDP80-R01731R000400360002-1: 'Films in China' in 'CIA Bulletin' (7 December 1960).

CIA-RDP82–00457R000300360008-5: 'Political Information: Communists in Hong Kong' (4 January 1947).

CIA-RDP82–00457R002300400004-2: 'Economic Information: Chinese Communist Procurement Activities in Hong Kong' (10 February 1949).

CIA-RDP82–00457R002800260006-1: 'Movement of Chinese Communists and Sympathizers From Hong Kong to Communist Controlled Areas' (6 June 1949).

CIA-RDP82–00457R002900650006-7: 'Attitude of Kuomintang (KMT) in Thailand toward Communist Victory in China' (28 July 1949).

CIA-RDP82–00457R004200330004-9: 'Interests of Communists in Canton and Hong Kong in Possible Labour Disturbances in Hong Kong and Macao' (24 January 1950).

CIA-RDP82–00457R005200230008-5: 'Kuomintang Attempts to Nullify Third Party Movements' (11 July 1950).

CIA-RDP82–00457R005400680009-3: '1. OMSNC Ships in Hong Kong 2. Communist Shipment From Hong Kong to Tientsin' (7 August 1950).

CIA-RDP82–00457R005500290006-8: '1. Hong Kong Currency. 2. Chinese Communist Purchases, Hong Kong' (8 August 1950).

CIA-RDP82–00457R006200670004-0: '1. Chinese Communist Intentions Toward Hong Kong 2. Chinese Military Activity in Kwuntung Province' (9 November 1950).

CIA-RDP82–00457R006200710001-8: 'Chinese Communist Message to Refugees in Hong Kong' (15 November 1950).

CIA-RDP82–00457R006500420012-8: '1. Chinese Communist Purchases in Hong Kong 2. Shipments from Hong Kong to Chinese Mainland' (13 December 1950).

CIA-RDP82–00457R006700210007-2: '1. Chinese Communist Commercial Activities and Firms', 2. From Hong Kong and Macao' (19 January 1951).

CIA-RDP82–00457R008000290002-4: 'Chinese Communist Terrorist Activities in the Hong Kong/Kowloon Area' (17 August 1951).

CIA-RDP82–00457R008500400005-3: '1. Chinese Communist Military Activities in Southern China 2. Chinese Communist Naval Activities' (1 September 1951).

CIA-RDP82–00457R008900210011-3: 'Activities of Chinese Communists in Hong Kong' (23 October 1951).

CIA-RDP89-B00569R000800020002-3: 'Preliminary Evaluation of Mission 3241 Flown in 16 November 1963' (20 November 1963).

CIA-RDP80R01362A000200100001-6: 'Impact of the U.S. Stand on Human Rights' (11 May 1977).

CIA-RDP83-00415R000200090029-8: 'Political Information: The International Society for the Defense of Human Rights' (24 February 1947)

Legislation

Hong Kong

Chinese Collaborators (Surrender) Ordinance 1947.
Explosive Substances Ordinance (Cap 206) 1913 (amended 1950).

Books

Alexander, Bevin. *The Strange Connection: The U.S. Intervention in China 1944–1972* (New York: Greenwood Press, 1992).

American Consulate General (Hong Kong). *Chinese Press Review* (Hong Kong: American Consulate General, 1956).

Bianco, Lucien. *Origins of the Chinese Revolution 1915–1949* (Stanford: Stanford University Press, 1967).

Bolton, K. and Hutton, C. *Triad Societies: Triad Societies in Hong Kong* (London: Taylor & Francis, 2000).

Brugger, Bill. *China: Liberation and Transformation 1942–1962* (London: Croom Helm, 1981).

CCP, China Handbook Editorial Committee. *History* (Peking: Foreign Languages Press, 1982).

Chesneaux, Jean. *Peasant Revolts in China 1840–1949* (London: Thames and Hudson, 1973).

Chi-kwan, Mark. *The Everyday Cold War: Britain and China 1950–1972* (London: Bloomsbury, 2017).

Chu, Cindy. *Chinese Communists and Hong Kong Capitalists 1937–1997* (New York: Palgrave Macmillan, 2010).

Dikötter, Frank. *The Age of Openness: China Before Mao* (Los Angeles: University of California, 2008).

Flett, Keith (ed). *A History of Riots* (Newcastle: Cambridge Scholars Publishing, 2015).

Fraser, George MacDonald. *Flashman and the Dragon* (London: Harper Collins, 1999).

Freemantle, Anne (ed). *Mao Tse-tung: An Anthology of His Writings* (New York: Mentor, 1962).

Goh, Chor Boon. *Technology and Entrepot Colonialism in Singapore* (Singapore: Institute of South East Asian Studies, 2013).

Hu Sheng. *Imperialism and Chinese Politics* (Peking: Foreign Languages Press, 1955).

James, Lawrence. *The Rise and Fall of the British Empire* (London: Abacus, 1994).

Jones, Carol and Vagg, John. *Criminal Justice in Hong Kong* (Oxford: Routledge, 2007).

Kafka, Franz. *The Great Wall of China: Stories and Reflections* (New York: Schocken Books: 1946).

Laqueur, Walter. *No End to War: Terrorism in the Twenty-First Century* (New York: Continuum, 2004).

Lao Tzu. *Tao Te Ching* (London: Penguin Classics, 1963).

Lifton, Robert Jay. *Revolutionary Immortality: Mao Tse-tung and the Chinese Cultural Revolution* (London: Weidenfeld, 1968).

Loh, Christine. *Underground Front: The Chinese Communist Party in Hong Kong* (Hong Kong: Hong Kong University Press, 2010).

Mao. *Quotations from Chairman Mao Tse-tung* (London: Transworld Publishers, 1967).

Morgan, W.P. *Triad Societies: Triad Societies in Hong Kong* (London: Routledge, 2000).

Naylor, R.T. *Hot Money and the Politics of Debt* (Montreal: MacGill-Queens University Press, 2004).

Paoli, Letizia (ed). *The Oxford Handbook to Organised Crime* (Oxford: Oxford University Press, 2014).

Rodzinski, Witold. *The People's Republic of China: A Concise Political History* (New York: Free Press, 1989).

Salisbury, Harrison. *New Emperors: Mao and Deng* (London: Harper Collins, 1992).

Wong, Ting-hong. *Hegemonies Compared: State Formation and Chinese School Politics in Postwar Singapore and Hong Kong* (New York: Routledge, 2002).

Chapters in books

Birchall, Ian. 'Imagined Violence: Some Riots in Fiction' in Keith Flett (ed), *A History of Riots* (Newcastle: Cambridge Scholars Publishing, 2015).

Chung-fun Hung. 'Interest Groups and Democracy Movement in Hong Kong: A Historical Perspective' in Sonny Shiu Hing Lo (ed), *Interest groups and the New Democracy Movement in Hong Kong* (Oxon: Routledge, 2018), 26.

Duara, Prasenjit. 'Provincial Narratives of the Nation: Centralism and Federalism in Republican China' in Harumi Befu (ed), *Cultural Nationalism in East Asia: Representation and Identity* (Berkeley: Institute of East Asian Studies, 1993).

Freilich, Robert. 'The Emerging General Theory of Civil Disobedience Within the Legal Order' in Richard Chikorta and Michael Moran (eds), *Riot in the Cities: An Analytical Symposium on the Causes and Effects* (Rutherford: Fairleigh Dickinson University Press, 1970).

Lombardo, Johannes. 'A Mission of Espionage, Intelligence and Psychological Operations: The American Consulate 1949–1964' in Richard Aldrich, Gary Rawnsley and Ming Yen Rawnsley (eds), *The Clandestine Cold War in Asia* (New York: Frank Cass, 2000).

Purdy, Jemma. 'The "Other" May Riots: Anti-Chinese Violence in Solo, May 1998' in Charles Coppel (ed), *Violent Conflicts in Indonesia: Analysis, Representation, Resolution* (London: Routledge, 2006).

Tang, James. 'World War to Cold War: Hong Kong's Future and Anglo-Chinese Interactions, 1941–55' in Ming Chan (ed), *Precarious Balance Hong Kong Between China and Britain 1842–1992* (Hong Kong: Hong Kong University Press, 1994).

Wilkinson, Paul. 'Pathology and Theory' in Walter Laqueur (ed), *The Terrorism Reader: A Historical Anthology* (London: Wildwood House, 1979).

Young, John. 'The Building Years: Maintaining a China-Hong Kong-Britain Equilibrium, 1950–1971' in Ming Chan (ed), *Precarious Balance Hong Kong Between China and Britain 1842–1992* (Hong Kong: Hong Kong University Press, 1994).

Journal articles

Miners, Norman. 'Plans for Constitutional Reform in Hong Kong 1946–1952 and 1984–1989' *Asian Journal of Public Administration* vol. 11, no. 1 (1997).

Tsang, Steve. 'Strategy for Survival: The Cold War and Hong Kong's Policy Toward Kuomintang and Chinese Communist Activities in the 1950s' *Journal of Imperial and Commonwealth History* vol. 25, no. 2 (2008).

Wesley-Smith, Peter. 'Chinese Consular Representation in British Hong Kong' *Pacific Affairs* vol. 71, no. 3 (2003).

Newspapers/periodicals

Brown, Anthony. 'The Societies Specialise in Violence' *The Canberra Times* (7 August 1964).

Dennen, Leon. 'Eyewitness Report: "Frightful Reign of Terror" in Red China' *New York World – Telegram and Sun* (28 July 1951).

Editorial. 'Overseas Chinese' *Ta Kung Pao* (28 January 1950).

Michison, Lois. 'Hong Kong Riots' *New Statesman and Nation* (20 October 1956).

Shaplen, Robert. 'Guerrillas – Our Hope in Red China' *Collier's* (21 July 1951).

Internet

David Bandurski, 'Hurting the Feelings of the Zhao Family' Avail at: http://chinamediaproject.org/2016/01/29/hurting-the-feelings-ofthe-zhao-family/ (accessed: 8 August 2018)

Dykes, Godfrey, Godfrey Dykes personal website. 'Hong Kong–October 1956' (no date). Avail at: www.godfreydykes.info/HONG%20KONG%201956.pdf (accessed: 14 January 2018).

HKPF, Hong Kong Police Website. 'The Modern Era'. Avail at: www.police. gov.hk/info/doc/history/chapter02_en.pdf (accessed: 3 September 2018).

Industrial History Group. 'Industrial History of Hong Kong' (18 July 2018). Avail. at: https://industrialhistoryhk.org/garden-company-%E5%98%89%E 9%A0%93%E6%9C%89%E9%99%90%E5%85%AC%E5%8F%B8-founded-1926/ (accessed: 10 August 2018).

Liu Xiaobo. 'In Full: Charter 08 Liu Xiaobo's Pro-democracy Manifesto for China That Led to His Jailing' (14 July 2017). Avail. at: www.hongkongfp. com/2017/07/14/full-charter-08-liu-xiaobos-pro-democracy-manifesto-china-led-jailing/ (accessed: 29 March 2018).

Index

For Product Safety Concerns and Information please contact our
EU representative GPSR@taylorandfrancis.com Taylor & Francis
Verlag GmbH, Kaufingerstraße 24, 80331 München, Germany